CLARENCE P.

Disreputable tales from Portsmouth Poly

By Jonathon Hopkins

1

Contents

Chapter 1 – Star of India

I think my sister was worried I had joined the Moonies, or some such cultish organisation.

"You seem to be making a lot of payments to them," she complained when I made an initial trip back home after my first few months of study at Portsmouth Polytechnic.

It probably wasn't the best idea to have my student bank account at the same branch of NatWest that my twin worked for. It meant that she could easily keep a close eye on my finances, which was both a good thing and a bad thing – particular as, being the lovely girl that she is, she would quite regularly deposit some of her wages into my account to keep me from going overdrawn.

"I can't have the branch manager writing to you to complain about your account," she used to say. Although I was always threatening to come in myself and have a talk to her boss about the iniquity of the charges levied on me and the evils of the whole banking system.

I never did, of course, I didn't really want to embarrass her or get her the sack. I confined myself to muttering darkly in Marks & Spencer – another institution I had taken against (even though I still bought all my underwear and socks from its stores) – which my mother found infuriating.

But Sian was definitely concerned by the regular payments of around £10 to £20 which I was paying out to "The Star of India" on a more than weekly basis. In her mind I was being fleeced by some Far Eastern mind controlling organisation, where in reality – of course – I was just eating far too many curries after a big session down the pub.

Although curry was something my mother made at home occasionally – normally as a way of using up the turkey leftovers at Christmas – we had never as a family visited an Indian restaurant. Indeed trips for meals out were normally limited to special occasions like the last nights of holidays, theatre trips, or birthdays. My parents were not frugal, but they did try and budget to their limited resources as best they could and that ideal had been passed down to my sister and I. That is until I went to college.

I was the first member of my immediate family to get the opportunity to study – although my mother's cousins were very academic and two of them had even gone to Oxford. However, I still went a convoluted way about it.

My sister and I both managed to flunk our 'A' levels, meaning that entry to a university – let alone Oxbridge – was not going to happen, but I had managed to apply for the back-up of a place at a Polytechnic – then the lower level of academic institutions. My grades, however, were even below the entry offer I had initially got from Portsmouth, so any thought of my leaving home for any glittering spires looked less than zero.

Instead, I knuckled down, found myself a job and prepared to labour on for what I expected to be the next, nigh on, fifty years of my working life! Thereby leaving academia to another generation of the Hopkins family.

However, a few months into my stint as a Mortgage Administration Clerk at the Greenwich Building Society I received a letter from the tutor who had interviewed me for a place at Portsmouth Poly enquiring why I had failed to take up my place on the 'Historical Studies' course. I wrote back apologising for not informing him that I wouldn't be taking up the college place, but that as my two 'D' grade 'A' levels were far below the two 'B's' that my offer required I had assumed I would have automatically been rejected.

My next communication from Dr Ken Lunn – who would go on to be my main supporter on the course staff at Portsmouth – asked me to give him a call and said that if I would still like to they could make a course place available to me for the following academic year.

I was stunned, and a little confused. Never having been the best when it came to making choices – as a child I would often end up with no sweets because my parents got infuriated at my inability to decide between the Black Jacks and the Fruit Salads (though luckily my sister always shared hers with me!) – I weighed up the options in my mind. Fifty years of slaving over a Mortgage Redemption Statement as opposed to three years of reading lots of books, living away from home, and partying non-stop? I can't believe I took so long to make up my mind.

Obviously I had to talk over this big decision with my parents, because they would effectively have to fund me for the following three years. Although we did apply through the local council for a full Student Grant - which in those days would pay for your accommodation, food and living, and sundries – we were only allocated the minimum level as my parents income was deemed too high, even though they really seemed to have very little to spare each month. Mind you, I should not have complained of course, because we didn't have to take out any Student loans or have to pay ridiculously expensive course fees ourselves back in the 1980's – I have no idea how today's student cope.

However, despite the expenses worries, my parents were very keen for me to take up the Portsmouth offer and blaze a trail as the first academic in our family, and having spoken to Dr Lunn I accepted his kind offer and said I would be happy to come down to Portsmouth for the start of the Autumn term in 1983.

I, of course, had to tell my employer of my decision, and thought it best to let them know sooner rather than later. So, just three months in to my building society career I summoned the courage to tell them that I would be ending it in nine months time, with the worry that they could just show me the door straight away. As it was the chief executive, Robin Nichols very kindly agreed that I could stay on for the full period, although he added that they would be sad to see me go as I had proved an exemplary member of staff (I'm not sure he was saying that ten months on, however!)

So the stage was set, I just had to crack on and amass some savings for my big Portsmouth adventure, focus my mind on the world of Historical Studies and get through some of the reading lists before the September start.

The best laid plans, of course, often fail, however, and given my salary was fairly meagre – I have kept my first P60 from the Greenwich Building Society and my annual wage was the equivalent of what I now pay in tax for one month! – there was not a lot of saving getting done. I probably had enough to get through my first term at Poly, but after that the council grant and my parents' contributions would have to keep me going.

Hence, why my sister would keep a close eye on my bank account, and why I really should not have been eating out quite so often in 'The Star of India' restaurant.

Come September, I was unable to get a place in one of the Poly's Halls of Residence and was instead allocated a room in lodgings at the far end of Southsea, down near the Canoe Lake and not far from the beach and pier.

The property was a big four storey, imposing Victorian red brick house on Nettlecombe Avenue run by a landlady – whose name I unfortunately can't recall – whose husband was in the Navy and rarely at home. She lived there with her 16-year old daughter, a real Lolita who would saunter through the dining area for us students in a fleecy dressing gown on her way to the family bathroom which was downstairs by the kitchen, drawing the eyes of the three males, including me. I remember she had a 6 foot 5 inch tall older boyfriend who was on the local ice hockey team and would glower at us menacingly.

There were seven students in all living in Nettlecombe Avenue – four girls sharing two rooms, as well as the three boys, one of whom had a single room - but that wasn't me! I got to share a room at the back on the second floor, but luckily it was with a really cool guy from York who was even doing the same course as me.

Yorkie, as of course he became known, was also – like me - a bit older than the majority of the students who had mostly come straight from school, and had worked for a while at the Rowntree factory in his home city. This meant he also had a large selection of sweets and chocolates to woo the girls - and me.

However, the supply of confectionery was short-lived as he only stayed in the house on Nettlecombe Avenue – and indeed in Portsmouth – for a fortnight. Within a few days of starting the Historical Studies course, he was informed that he had also been accepted for the University of York, and it was a no brainer that he move back to his home city and take up that place instead.

I, of course, would miss him, but the good news was that I would get to have the big room to myself – well at least until the landlady found another student to take his place.

The other male student in the lodgings was someone I would get to know well over the years at Portsmouth, not least because he would also occupy the iconic flat at Clarence Parade (which gives this memoir its title) in our second year at the Poly. Richard 'Mad Guitar' Axton was a very self-effacing student on a biosciences course. He was from Woking in Surrey; claimed a family link to Country music star Hoyt Axton; and was a gifted guitar player himself – hence the soubriquet. I would often go to sleep at night listening to him perfect the playing of Led Zeppelin's classic 'Stairway to Heaven' and then wake up in the morning to hear the same tune being played again – I was never sure whether he had been doing that all night!

Life in Nettlecombe Avenue was fairly quiet and ordered, which suited me fine, particularly when I had a room to myself. The four girls were always running around, giggling amongst themselves and making themselves up for parties and other nights out, but they rarely disturbed Richard and I – indeed they rarely noticed us. They mostly had established boyfriends who would come and visit them, and indeed I had left a girlfriend back home whom I kept in contact with and who came down to visit me during that first term, and whom I would see on the couple of occasions when I returned to Bromley.

Karen was one of the mixed Venture Scout pack I had joined a year or two earlier with my sister, having both graduated though the Cubs and the Scouts, and the Brownies and the Guides respectively. I very much enjoyed my time Scouting, and realistically all my formative experiences came wearing the scarf and the woggle – drinking my first pint of beer, smoking a cigarette (and a joint), and learning more about girls! I certainly remember "swapping woggles" with a bunch of Swedish girl scouts on a camping trip to Luxembourg!

The experiences with the West Wickham Venture Scouts were just as interesting, as they were a really nice bunch of people, and we all tended to go on holidays together, to the likes of Cornwall and Jersey, rather than any extreme camping trips. There was inevitably some pairing up between the sexes given the ages, and I had made a move on the lovely Karen just a month or so before heading down to Portsmouth – which wasn't the best of timing.

She was a year or so younger than me and just finishing school, so it wasn't easy to keep the flame going when I upped sticks and headed down to the South Coast, but we tried our best. It helped that she had relatives that lived quite close to Portsmouth who she came down to visit one weekend and managed to stay over at my lodgings on the Saturday night. It required some subterfuge, but she claimed to be staying with a girl friend she had met, and I sneaked her in through the side stairs into my lodgings without the landlady knowing, so we spent some time alone together – helped by my having the room to myself.

That situation did not last long, however, and half-way through the first term, another student arrived to share my room, having been recommended by one of the girls in the lodgings who had known him from home. Angus was far from quiet and self-effacing like Richard Axton, he was a tall, clumsy type of guy, pretty loud and use to living alone. He did not adapt well to room-sharing.

Perhaps the main bone of contention was his clock-radio-tape-player, which he used to set for 7am (breakfast being at 8am) and which would wake me up to the horrendous sound of Jethro Tull's 'Aqualung' album every morning – infinitely worse than Richard Axton's repetitive guitar-playing.

Having a room-mate also meant there was no way Karen could spend another furtive night at my lodgings, and indeed she never came back down to Portsmouth to see me. We muddled through together over the Christmas break, but a month or so in to my second term at Portsmouth, the relationship came to an end. Karen was finding it hard having a long-distance boyfriend and worried that I was enjoying student life too much, so she broke things off, which saddened me but was probably for the best.

To be honest, although I was most certainly not getting myself involved with any other girls down in Portsmouth – and indeed went around for a long period calling myself celibate (in the forlorn hope that it might spark more female interest!) - my life was definitely changing as a student and my interests and desires were shifting.

Chapter 2 - Economic History

have always called the Historical Studies course I did at Portsmouth a 'drinking degree'. It helped that there were only a few hours of lectures and seminars a week to attend, with the rest of the time supposed to be spent reading in the library and writing long essays, but that mostly meant plenty of time to enjoy oneself in pubs and the Student Union bar.

The stage was set early on, indeed the preliminary lecture in the department building at King's Rooms ended with the lecturers taking the new students on a pub crawl to Old Portsmouth, culminating in a pleasant few hours spent drinking Horndean Special Bitter (HSB) in the lovely 'Still & West' overlooking the harbour.

It was here I talked to my course mates for the first time, and - aside from Yorkie who, as I have mentioned, would only be around a very short time – it was here I met up with most of the people who would remain my closest friends throughout my three years down in Portsmouth, and some for a long time after.

It was perhaps not a major surprise that three of the guys I most hit it off with all came from around London – indeed one of them was actually also from Bromley, and another came from the next-door borough of Croydon. The latter,

Chris Taylor, actually became known as The Man from Croydon - which was shortened to Manfred and sometimes Manf - because we didn't catch his real name at the time. Indeed Mark – the other guy from Bromley – and myself are the only people still calling Chris 'Manf' when we meet up for a beer or two nowadays, with other people looking at us strangely as a result.

The other London-domiciled student would perhaps have the biggest influence on my time at Portsmouth, given that we would both choose to live in digs together for the majority of our three years down there – including in Clarence Parade. Rod Constanti was a good-looking guy, into music, politics and enjoying himself, capable of attracting the girls and organising the entertainments. He could be unreliable and infuriating at times, but was always fun and a ready source of drink, drugs, and party people.

When he first suggested we get a flat to share together at the end of our second term at Portsmouth I jumped at the idea, keen to escape the confines of Nettlecombe Avenue and sharing a room with Jethro Tull fan Angus. The reality, of course, was that we ended up sharing a one-room bedsit in a run-down flat on Shaftesbury Avenue which had no bathroom – just one shared toilet – and which made my mother cry all the way back to Bromley after she and my father had dropped my belongings off there for the first time after Easter. Thankfully my sister never saw it!

It was, of course, supremely cheap, meaning that we had lots of cash to spare for the essentials of student life – pints of beer, late night curries, trips to Caesars nightclub, and various types of drugs! And, indeed, that was the pattern our life followed.

The nearest decent pub to the flat and to the King's Rooms, where we infrequently had to attend lectures, was the India Arms, which served the lovely HSB and was invariably packed with students we knew. From there it was only a short stagger after closing time to 'The Star of India' curry house for a vindaloo or a phall, and on a Thursday or Friday a longer walk down to the seafront for the nightclubs and late-bars around and on the pier.

There was occasional drinking in the Students Union, which had the advantage of a subsidised bar, but the disadvantage of always being packed, and lunchtime drinking was not something that happened too often – maybe only ahead of an afternoon lecture – as mostly we would still be crashed out in our flat after the big night out and then preparing ourselves for doing it all over again.

However, there was one – unfortunately – memorable lunchtime drinking session in the Students Union during our second term at the Poly. Certainly my fellow Historical Studies students remember it all too well, while I do my best to try and forget it! It gave me a unique record – as I became the first student to throw-up in a lecture (and not be expelled!)

It was the first lecture for a new module on 'Economic History' to be delivered by an elderly lady who none of us had ever met before. It coincided, however, with the arrival for me that morning of a letter from Karen – my long distance girlfriend – calling an end to our near six month relationship. I should not have been surprised, given that we had spent most of that time not seeing each other, but I was still upset as I had some deep feelings and would miss hearing from her.

It was in this depressed state that I rendezvoused with Rod and others of the Historical Studies crew in the bar of the Students Union, which was only a short walk from our lecture venue, to drown my sorrows ahead of the 'Economic History' afternoon.

I proceeded to that drowning in very swift fashion and made my way through at least six pints of HSB in the hour or so before we needed to make our way to King's Rooms. This was small beer for a normal student evening drinking session but was far too much to consume ahead of an afternoon's lecture on an empty stomach. Consequently, when the time to leave came, all my friends were telling me that it was not a very good idea to go along.

Of course, I felt fine, and argued that I could not miss the first class of a new course, so I staggered to my feet and joined the crowd making their way over to the lecture rooms. Rod was similarly intoxicated but he had the good sense to remain behind in the Students Union.

Making our way into the lecture room, I had to rely on my fellow students to help steer me to a desk at the back of the class, where I proceeded to place my head down on my arms on the table. People, especially the girls, were looking at me with worried expressions on their faces, but before anyone could say anything, the new lecturer entered the room and took up her place at the front of the class.

I am sure she must have noticed the student slumped at the back, but she carried on with the introductions to herself and the new course, handing round a sheaf of notes and booklists. Not that I, of course, noticed anything. Once the class had settled down, and all had received the necessary papers, the lecturer – who I am sure was called Ena, but I have no idea of her surname – asked the first, memorable question:

"What does anyone know about economic history?"

That was my cue to chunder. I don't think I even lifted my head of my arms, but just threw up on the desk, though of course I don't remember anything.

Ena the lecturer was, understandably, horrified by this turn of events in her first lecture with a new bunch of students, and was frozen to the spot. However, luckily, my saviour, Dr Ken Lunn entered the room about the same time, delivering a stand with a TV and video for the class to enjoy.

Although equally as horrified, he took charge of the situation and told 'Fascist' Mark and another friend to get hold of me and help me out of the room. Unfortunately on the way I managed to throw up a bit more over the TV and video stand before they managed to steer me through the door and get me downstairs to the toilets. After helping clean me up a bit, Mark volunteered to take me up to his room in Rees Hall – right next door to the King's Rooms – to let me recover. Ken Lunn agreed that this would be the best course of action, and between them they helped me upstairs.

I remember trying to shake hands with Dr Lunn as he left me in Mark's charge, and then I was left to sleep off the effects of my lunchtime session. Luckily, the teaching staff never got to know what had caused me to disgrace myself in a lecture, as my friends had all suggested that it must have been something I ate!

I was, of course, mortified, when I had recovered and been told of my disgraceful behaviour. I had to face Dr Lunn and explain myself – the previous night's curry of course being blamed! – and apologise to Ena the lecturer, who never gave me any decent markets for the economic history course (although that probably was because I was no good at it!)

I now make a living writing about financial markets, which of course necessitates understanding and interpreting economic data, however, I will never be allowed to forget my introduction to economic history in that lecture room at Portsmouth Poly.

Chapter 3 – Woking Wanders

The 'India Arms' was packed at the end of another lovely May day.

Rod and I sat in the back of the pub, near to the toilets, nursing our half-pints – HSB for me and some lager for him.

We weren't drunk, but were far from sober, and more importantly not at all stoned. The reason being that after some sort of police clampdown the supply of cannabis into Portsmouth had, for us, virtually dried up.

Given the proximity of our end of first year exams and associated stress, this was a really bad time not to be able to have a toke, and Rod, especially, was getting very jittery.

It was nearly closing time and the thought of returning to our single room digs with nothing to smoke when we got back was causing him to come up with various far-fetched plans to try and overcome the hashish drought.

"If I was back home in London, I could easily score some," my flat mate postulated. "Why don't we just head up to the smoke?"

I certainly cannot have been sober, because I seemed to think that, even at nearly 10.30 at night, that was an eminently sensible idea.

So what if we had some big revision seminars coming up in the next few days ahead of the exams, we could just hop a train up to London, score some hash and head back down to college, getting a day out in the capital into the bargain.

Rising slightly unsteadily to our feet, Rod and I drained our beers and headed across the pub towards the main door.

"Where you guys going?" a voice called out from the crowd around the bar. It was unmistakeably the Yorkshire twang of Eric the Vegan, a History course-mate and one of Rob's Militant recruits.

As we stopped to answer him, Eric made his way over towards us. As always he was wearing a long, shabby coat, even given the day's fair weather, and behind his thick spectacles he looked something like a mole.

"We are off to London to score some dope," said Rob, slightly sotto voice as he approached.

"Wow!", Eric replied, "That sounds fun. Can I come along?"

Rod and I looked at each other questioningly. We didn't really know Eric that well then. He'd always seemed quite a sensible guy – cooking with hash rather than smoking it – and we were both not sure what he would bring to the upcoming adventure.

However, we weren't going to be mean and say no, so with an incline of his head, Rod indicated that we should both follow him out of the pub door.

Once outside, we headed north towards Portsmouth & Southsea station near the centre of town. It was not a long walk, probably only 10 or 15 minutes from the India, past our lecture halls at the King's Rooms, and the Student Union and library.

We didn't bump into any of the crew who knew us on the way, or perhaps they might have talked us out of this late night flit.

When we got to the station, the platform was deserted as well, with good reason too as the last train to London had already left!

We consulted the timetables stuck up on the walls and there was just one other train due to depart before the station closed, but that was only going as far as Woking in Surrey, still a long way from the capital.

Woking. Home of The Jam – my favourite band growing up. The family home also of Richard 'Mad Guitar' Axton, the guy who shared my first digs with me in Southsea. It had to be a good place.

Rod suggested we hop on this last train, and then catch the milk train up in the morning from Woking to London, which would probably only mean spending a few hours cooling our heels in deepest Surrey.

There wasn't a long wait before the train pulled in to the platform, having started off at the Portsmouth Harbour station at the Hard. We jumped on board, obviously without having thought about getting anything like a ticket.

Not surprisingly there were few other people on board the train, and none at all in the carriage that we chose.

Rod and I settled in to a bank of four seats, and stretched out, preparing to get some shut eye for the two hour journey up to Woking, with the train set to make quite a few stops before we reached our initial destination.

Eric, however, being sensible, and a good Yorkshireman was conscious of the fact that we had boarded without any tickets, and that given the likelihood of a train conductor being on board, we should make sure we were always two steps ahead of the game.

As we were near the front of the train he headed back down the carriages to see if he could spot the ticket inspector and scope out where we could hide to avoid him.

These were the days of proper train carriages, with first class cubicles and corridors, and toilets that you could lock yourself in. Not like today's endless line of carriages with continuous access and automatic toilets with time-delayed doors.

He headed back after around 10 minutes having made it down to the last carriage, which was where the conductor had started the ticket inspection.

Rousing the two of us, Eric suggested that, as there were very few people on the train between us and the conductor, it might be a good idea for all three of us to lock ourselves in one of the lavatories.

Whilst this seemed a wise decision, Rod and I were not too enamoured with the idea of giving up our comfy seats to squeeze into the fouling smelling toilet.

However, both being without much in funds, and those we had being needed for scoring in London, we followed Eric a few carriages back to the first lavatory and locked the door. It was a pretty small space, so one of us sat on the toilet seat, another perched on the washbasin cupboard, and the third stretched out on the floor.

The window out of the train was, as always, frosted glass, so no one could see in on your ablutions and as we passed through deserted stations picking up speed, orange lights briefly glowed bright, and then disappeared again into darkness.

We had made the first of our scheduled stops, though we couldn't tell where, before there came the first bang on the lavatory door, with the conductor calling out for tickets.

None of us made a sound, all holding our breath as the banging came a second time before, after what seemed an age, we heard the train employee move on up the carriage.

With a sigh of relief, Rod got up off the floor and made to open the toilet door, but Eric swiftly stopped him and indicated he should resume his seat, pointing out that the conductor would return once he had got to the end of the train and then headed back to his post.

Rod wasn't happy about it, but there seemed no alternative and we settled in for the long trip ensconced in the lavatory.

Sure enough, ten minutes or so later there came another banging on the toilet door and another call for tickets, but once again we stayed quiet and the conductor moved off this time with some audible grumbling but no further action.

Even in our far from comfortable accommodation, the three of us fairly soon nodded off as the journey continued, hypnotised by the passing lights and the stuffy atmosphere. Luckily none of us had drunk enough to require them to make full use of the facilities.

Eventually, there was a jerk to a halt and a call of 'Last stop, everyone off' from the conductor, who appeared to be on the station platform, albeit close by to our toilet window.

Stirring ourselves to quietly unlatch the door, and keeping down below window level we made our way back down the carriages to put some distance between ourselves and the train man.

Peaking out from a window up the platform, we could see the conductor get back on the train close to where our toilet shelter had been, and then there was a ring of the train bell, and another jerk, and we realised that if we didn't jump off soon, we would be heading down to the railway sidings for the night.

Opening the door just as the train started to pick up some speed, Rod threw himself out of the carriage, landing in a heap on the platform.

I followed, and just before the front of the train started to exit the station, Eric also managed to fling himself out, nearly rolling off the edge and on to the tracks.

The train door remained open, banging against the side of the carriage and the conductor stuck his head out of the window further back and shouted at us, but as he passed us by the train was gathering pace and we were scampering off down the deserted platform towards the sign marked exit.

There were no barriers, not like the ones you'd need to vault over nowadays, and no station workers, thankfully, were around either to challenge us. We had made it. At least to the first stage in our journey. The next part up to London we would have to endure later.

For now it was around 2am in Woking, and having consulted the station timetable we knew we had around a 2-1/2 hour wait until the first train up to London Waterloo departed in the morning.

Looking around us, we could see very little. It was a moonless night with the sky swathed in cloud, and there were no street lights around Woking station.

We could make out a parade of shops, some offices and a main road ahead of us, but all were quiet and deserted, with very little light around.

We headed for the road, not having much of a plan aside from to walk around Woking until the time arrived for us to board another train. This indeed was the only option as there certainly seemed very little else to do in the Surrey town in the wee small hours.

Once reaching the highway we looked up and down and randomly chose a direction to walk in. It was cold, but we had coats on so it was not too bad.

'Anyone got any fags left?', asked Rod.

I searched my pockets, but all I had was an empty packet containing only my Bic lighter.

Eric, however, managed to retrieve the remains of a roll-up from his search, and what was more to the point it contained the last bits of weed he'd had left.

Fantastic, we could all have a hit.

We knelt down beside a hedge which separated the pavement from an office building of some sort to try and light the remnant out of the wind. My lighter was too feeble, but luckily Rod had his old Zippo, and after a few attempts he had got the mini-spliff lit.

He took the first drag and was just passing it on to Eric when some car lights came around the corner up ahead. Rod spotted the blue light on the top of the vehicle instantly and swiftly dived over the hedge to avoid being seen.

Eric and I just crouched down further and the police car carried quickly on its way with its occupants failing to be unsettled by our slightly strange behaviour.

After the vehicle had passed out of sight the two of us stood up and peered over the hedge to see where Rod had got to. He was lying on his back on the grass in front of the office building looking slightly sheepish.

"Has it gone?" he asked. Eric nodded and Rod got slowly to his feet.

"Where's the mini-spliff?" I asked, looking down at Rod's empty hands.

"Errr, I ditched it," he responded, pointing to a flower bed in front of the office's windows.

Eric, having joined Rod on the other side of the hedge, moved forward to search for the remains, but could find nothing among the bushes and flowers.

"Great!", I added. "You managed to have a toke, but we got nothing, and now you can't even find it!!"

Annoyed I turned my back on the pair of them, and headed down the road to walk off my anger. They soon caught me up with Rod apologising profusely.
The rest of the night passed by fairly quickly, however, with the three of us walking a loop around the outskirts of the centre of Woking before returning to the station only about 15 minutes before the first train was scheduled to arrive.

Once again there were no other people at the station, either passengers or railway staff, and as the so-called 'milk train' trundled in we were free to board the carriages once again without a ticket.

This time there was no conductor on board, or at least none that we saw, and the around half-hour journey passed quickly.

Before we knew it we were pulling into London Waterloo station, back in the big smoke and closer to our goal of scoring some drugs.

Chapter 4 – A Mars A Day

The opening bars of the Kinks' classic 'Waterloo Sunset' was running through all our heads as we stood on the bridge looking at the view of the sun coming up behind the never-slumbering city.

It was the wrong end of the day I know, but such a special moment deserved an iconic soundtrack. Rod and I were back in our home town and we were closer to being able to score some hash, and then head back down to Portsmouth in time for the next day's exam seminars.

Or that's what we thought as we stared out across the big brown river, and the dome of St Paul's and all the other buildings, with the rising sun shooting its rays of pink and orange and gold into the early morning sky.

The reality, however, was to prove very different.

Rod had tried calling some of his mates in east London from Waterloo station as soon as we had managed to extricate ourselves from the train and somehow avoided the ticket collectors at the platform gates.

Perhaps not surprisingly, given that it was around six in the morning, none of Rod's mate were picking up, so we had to decide what we were going to do until he could get hold of them.

It looked like it was going to be a beautiful early summer day, and we were happy to spend it walking around the

capital, seeing some sites, having a beer or two a
waiting to meet Rod's friends.

Continuing over Waterloo Bridge we headed up towa.
Covent Garden, looking for an open café where we cou
get ourselves a cup of tea or coffee and a roll or
something for breakfast.

It was by now past seven o'clock and there was already a
steady flow of commuters also crossing the bridge, suited,
booted and ready for the working day.

It reminded me of my year of work in Greenwich, though I
hadn't had to commute by train to the building society's
head office, as I was able to drive there in the trusty
Vauxhall Viva my twin and I shared.

Luckily Sian worked slightly closer to our home near
Lower Sydenham and was able to get the train to her
bank's office in Elmers End, which was only three stops
away, so I had use of the car all the time.

If I hadn't driven I would have had to get the train all the
way into London Bridge and then caught another one back
out again to the Thames-side Royal Borough.

That would have taken almost an hour, whereas driving
across south-east London to Greenwich, even on the
traffic-heavy South Circular route, only took me around
half-an-hour.

I had enjoyed my time at the building society. Everyone
else, including my sister, had hedged their bets and
applied for the banks, which was seen as the best option
for post-A level employment.

Having managed to miss the closing dates for such
applications, I instead turned to applying for the bank's

'r cousins – the building societies. And as
s one of the nearer ones to have their head
ɥ them first.

ɥcted to get an interview, and was
ɥu get the right grades anyway to head to
ɥven before I had heard back from them.

ʋut luckily, as those A level grades were so abysmal, I had breezed through the interview with the kindly old lady and was offered a position with the MAD team – Mortgage Administration Department.

It turned out the kindly old lady was actually a bit hard-nosed and everyone was surprised she had chosen me over some easily better qualified candidates.

It turned out, however, that her son worked as a teacher at my old school, Langley Park Grammar in Beckenham, and he had even tutored me in English for a term or too. I doubt he would have been able to give me much of a reference, but just being at the same school helped.

Anyway, I quickly settled into working life in the small and pleasant team, dealing with jobs which played to my OCD organisational skills, such as filing and sending out notifications of changes in mortgage interest rates. Being the 1980's there were plenty of those, with rates getting hiked steadily by the Bank of England, hitting highs of around 15%, I remember.

They really were lovely and kind people to work for and being only a small society I got to do lots of different tasks in the various branch offices – particularly after I decided to revive my offer from Portsmouth.

That made me an asset that could be used across the business, and I found myself working anywhere that needed cover, driving around in either the little building society van, or if that wasn't available the chief executive's Audi!

The most memorable moment of that early job was also the most dangerous, when myself and my colleague were mugged while traversing a zebra crossing to deposit the previous day's takings into the nearby bank.

David Goggins, who was even younger than I was having left school at 16 to join the building society – where his Mum, Pat worked as the tea lady, among other things – was in charge of the leather bag containing the cash that morning, and I was his escort.

Perhaps it wasn't the best idea to entrust such an important task to two teenagers, but we had done it regularly over the months, following the same routine – which was probably our undoing.

Amusingly, just before we set off across the busy Greenwich High Road to get to the bank, Dave had been telling me about the karate class he had taken the night before and was showing me some of his moves if we were ever attacked.

In the event though, when it happened Dave just remained frozen to the spot near the traffic island in the middle of the road as the man wearing a balaclava in May held a knife to my throat and told him to hand over the bag.

My colleague remained static despite the situation and I had to say to him in a trembling voice: "Dave, hand over the money."

He came back to life, stretched out his hand, the bag was snatched from him and the robber was off like a rat up a drainpipe, shooting across the busy High Road traffic and disappearing down Creek Road behind the building society before Dave and I had even had a chance to turn and look.

We were still gaping at the disappearing robber when a car horn honked loudly in front of us. The impatient driver had turned in to the side road and had no idea what had just happened to us, so was trying to get us to quit the zebra crossing.

Dave and I retreated back across the road to the pavement where we had come from to find a big batch of Japanese tourists waiting to cross, none of whom had witnessed the robbery either, or certainly were not able to communicate much to us. They just wanted to know where was the Cutty Sark!

We pointed them in the right direction and sheepishly crossed the main road and went back into the building society where the chief cashier spotted that we were both as white as sheets and let us in through the side door into the office.

Ushered in to the society secretary's office, we shakily told our story and the police were called. Dave's Mum fussed around us and bought us both a cup of tea, and then we were taken up to Greenwich police station to give our statements.

Both Dave and I were taken to separate rooms to relate our testimonies, and it was pretty clear the policemen interviewing us were not at all convinced that we did not have anything ourselves to do with the robbery, even though I had a little nick on my neck where the knife had been tightly held at my throat.

I can't blame them, it was all pretty suspicious. There were no witnesses aside from the two of us. We had left the building society with the bag – which contained around £10,000 in cash – and had returned without it.

We could easily have made the robbery up, and stashed the bag somewhere, or thrown it into a friend's car who then drove off. It didn't help that I had already quit my sensible job to become a feckless student in a few months time so was probably in need of cash.

The questioning went on for most of the morning and into lunchtime although, as both Dave and I continued to repeat the same story, after a while the policemen decided to let us go back to the office. I think the fact that my father was in the Metropolitan Police also helped to overcome some of the suspicion that had fallen on me.

Mr Borrett, the building society secretary – number two in power to the CEO – was very kind and let us both go home for the afternoon. Although whether that was because the police wanted to have us followed to see if we both met up after, or with someone else, and led them to the money, who knows.

Certainly the robbery investigation continued for a good few months, and Dave and I were called back to the police station a number of times to go over our stories. No one was ever caught, but my student lifestyle certainly didn't indicate that I was flush with cash.

Now I was back in London, watching the commuters, and was far from envious of their lives, even if they probably had a lot more money than me. At least I had enough for the cup of tea and bacon roll that would be my reward when we found a decent café.

I have always liked the area around the Covent Garden piazza, even though it is a massive tourist trap, as there are still some good old traditional shops, restaurants and boozers, if you know where to look.

Rod led us to a greasy spoon he knew not far from Maiden Lane and we settled down to enjoy our breakfast. On the way we had picked up a newspaper to share – not unsurprisingly the left-leaning 'Guardian' – and 20 Marlboro to enjoy after our repast.

Every so often, Rod would disappear off to the phone box at the end of the road to call his mates, but even when he eventually managed to track some of them down, none of them were in a position to help us score some hash.

It was looking like our journey was going to prove fruitless, with Rod's well-lauded London contacts failing to deliver the goods, when Eric pulled a rabbit out of the hat with an even more audacious plan.

By this time it was about midday and having wandered around the capital for a few hours, browsing in bookshops, and record stores, the three of us were now ensconced in a pub in the Seven Dials area sipping half pints of warm beer and contemplating our disappointment.

"Chris said Swindon is the drug capital of the UK," piped up Eric. "Let's go there!"

Rod and I looked at each other quizzically, and then back at Eric. Swindon! The Wiltshire town around 100 miles down the M4 motorway, famous only for being the WH Smith shops distribution centre – I had had a Saturday job at the Bromley store so I knew this useless piece of information.

"How on earth would we get to Swindon?" said Rod. "And if we got there how and where would we find any contacts for us to score?"

Eric had thought of that though.

"Chris is actually at home on a study week. I have his phone number. He'll know the right people to contact to get us some gear," said the ingenious Yorkshireman.

Though still sceptical, Rod and I told Eric to go and give Chris a call and see what was possible, while we got in another round of drinks and a packet of pork scratchings for sustenance.

A beaming Eric came back about 20 minutes later. He had got through to Chris straight away and the older student was pretty enthusiastic about us making the trip down to Swindon, claiming he could deliver us some excellent hash.

Eric had already asked Chris about how to get to him in Swindon and had agreed we'd get a coach from Victoria around 4pm which should get us to the Wiltshire town around 6pm. Chris would meet us at the bus station there to take us back to the pub his parent's owned. Even more of a result.

Of course, all of this would mean there would be no way the three of us could be back in Portsmouth for the following morning's crucial exam seminar. But that would just have to be missed – the main issue was being able to get stoned.

As by now it was getting close to 2pm, and we weren't sure about the timing of buses and how to get the tickets at Victoria, the three of us downed our drinks, finished off the port scratchings, and headed for the tube.

It actually all proved pretty straightforward when we got to the coach station, with plenty of availability on the 4pm departure mentioned, and although the £15 fare made a dent in all our pockets, we still had enough cash left to pay for the hash and an evenings drinking.

Of course we'd then also have to get a coach down from Swindon to Portsmouth the next day, but that was another story.

The journey along the M4 to Swindon passed fairly easily, even though there was pretty of traffic at that time getting out of London, particularly as the three of us swiftly fell asleep on the back set we had commandeered.

Pretty close to the appointed time we were pulling into Swindon coach station, a non-descript concrete monstrosity, in a rather non-descript city centre, and there was Chris to meet us.

I didn't know him very well as he was a second year student, doing Cultural Studies rather than Historical Studies at Portsmouth. Eric and Rod knew him better as he was active in the college political societies.

I recognised him though, with his long flowing locks and round, John Lennon-style, old fashioned spectacles. I also remembered that he was a bit of a celebrity around the Poly as he had had some poems published in a literary magazine the previous summer.

He greeted us all warmly and indicated we should follow him to a nearby bus stop to make the journey to his parent's hostelry, on the other side of the city.

It didn't take us very long to reach 'The Red Lion' pub, a welcoming sight after our long day of travelling, and we headed into the saloon bar which was fairly quiet, with most of the locals drinking in the public bar next door. Chris's parents were not around, leaving the running of the bar to a manager and his staff who were happy to leave the three of us to our own devices.

We lined up some drinks and headed out into the empty beer garden where Chris pulled out of his pocket a very welcome sight – a big joint. Lighting it, he took a big drag and then passed it on to Rod.

We each took our turn of the steadily burning reefer, drawing the heady smoke deeply into lungs as if it was the first time, which it seemed like having been out of dope for so long.

The hash was pretty smooth and burned well without the fizzles and pops of the grass we had been used to getting recently in Portsmouth. So fairly quickly we all started to get that slightly stoned feeling, when little talking is possible and contemplation of ones drink takes priority.

That peaceful feeling though was shattered by a shout from the open pub door to Chris.

"Here, mate, your muckers have arrived for you," bellowed the voice, which turned out to be the middle-aged bar lady.

Chris acknowledged her and got up to go greet his other friends who were heading out to join us. There were two guys, both in fairly hippy-looking outfits with long hair, and a young girl, tall and thin wearing a kaftan-style dress.

We were all introduced, though the names never stuck in my head, and after another joint was produced and smoked by us all, Rod asked the all-important question.

"So, how do we get hold of some of this stuff?"

One of the guys looked at Chris, and after a nod from him, asked what we were actually looking for.

Rod countered by asking what was actually available, and at what cost.

"Depends," the guy answered in a pretty deep, West country burr. "You could have some Leb, Black or Red? Or some Afghan Rocky, which would be cheaper?"

"I'd always go for the black," Rod responded. "How many ounces could we get for, say, £50?"

Having only £15 left in cash myself by this stage I wasn't sure where Rod was going to get that sort of money from but I was too stoned by then to be really bothered. "That would probably get you about 4 or 5 ounces," the West Country lad replied. "About the size of a Mars Bar. Would that do?"

A Mars Bar, I thought. Wow! I had only really dealt in small wraps of hash of about a quarter of an ounce, perhaps Oxo cube sized. Something that big sounded amazing.

"That would be brilliant," I said.

Rod was equally as enthusiastic and asked how quickly the delivery could be made, perhaps thinking that we could even make it back down to Portsmouth that night. Chris's two mates conferred, while the girl eyed up Rod. They thought that if we gave them the cash now, they could be back inside an hour with the goods.

It was around 7.30pm now, and although we had absolutely no idea about coaches back to the south coast, it still felt possible that we could get back there that night.

Rod beckoned Eric and I over, and in a low voice asked how much cash we all had. I offered up the £15 I had left, and it turned out Rod had even less than that, only around a tenner.

We both looked at Eric. He might have appeared a make-weight at the start of this trip, but he was turning out to be the game changer.

The canny Yorkshireman pulled out a scrunched up £20 note from his coat, smoothed it out and proffered it to Rod. We were a fiver short, but were sure the guys could still sort us out handsomely with the available cash.

Rod handed it over to them and they nodded. It wouldn't be a problem.

Both got up to go and we all stood, shook their hands and hoped for their swift return. The girl stayed, still making moon eyes at Rod, slightly to the annoyance of Chris, I thought.

"Lets get another beer in," said the published poet, "then we'll head up to my room upstairs and listen to some sounds while waiting for the guys to come back."

That sounded like a perfect plan and soon we were ensconced in Chris's bedroom, a sizable space, with an expensive hi-fi system, big posters of various bands plastered around the walls and a battered red leather sofa which we all squeezed on to – the girl opting for Rod's lap.

Pink Floyd was slipped on to the turntable and with the sound ratcheted up to loud, another joint was lit and passed around as beers were sipped and everyone seemed contented. Especially Rod!

It was only when the light inside the room started to dim, and having gone though a batch of Floyd LPs that we realised quite how late it was, with no sign of Chris's mates returning.

In actual fact it was well past 10pm, and just before the pub closing time when the two lads eventually turned up. Rod had been getting a bit jittery that they may have just scarpered with our cash, but Chris was reassuring, and when they did turn up, it was worth the wait.

From inside his jacket pocket, the guy who had brokered the deal pulled out a block of hash, wrapped in cling film, and most certainly the size of a Mars Bar.

It was handed round, smelt and squeezed and declared perfect.

Straight away Rod got to work skinning up a few joints using the wonderful block of Black Lebanese, to repay our hosts and his friends for their generosity and kindness in relieving our drought.

There were, of course, no thoughts of getting back down to Portsmouth or of making the first year exam revision seminars. We settled back smoked our way through a chunk of the bounty, and then passed out.

I remember waking up much later, stretched out on Chris's bedroom carpet, head wedged against a radiator, to the sound of static, and a record needle bumping against the out-groove mixed with some gentle snoring from Rod and the others.

Lying next to me was the Mars Bar sized lump of hash, slightly shaved back but still looking a very lovely sight.

Chapter 5 - Isle of Wight Excursion

The first-year exams were over. Whether I had passed them were in the hands of the gods and the whims of the lecturers marking them.

Was my preparation for the exams ideal? Probably not, especially given our Swindon excursion, missed seminars and constantly stoned demeanour thanks to the Mars Bar hash block.

Could I have done more studying? Of course. But they were out of the way and now we could concentrate on having fun until everyone returned home for the summer holidays.

The drugs pipeline was also flowing again, and a decision was made to have a night of celebration across the water – on the Isle of Wight!

The Saturday following everyone's final exam was picked and arrangements were made to meet up at the Hard – where the ferries departed from.

The aim had been to get the girls involved too, but for whatever reason – probably innate good sense – they cried off, leaving just five lads to travel across to Ryde.

It was a lovely sunny June day when we set off, so t-shirts and jeans and no jackets were de rigeur. A few spliffs, a line of speed, and half a bottle of Beneylin were taken before departure by most to oil the enjoyment, though, in addition, Rod had decided to drop a tab of LSD as well.

This was something I had yet to try. I actually would wait until Rod and I travelled to the Glastonbury music festival later that summer for my one and only trip. I found it too scary, its impact impossible to predict both from a time perspective and a weirdness factor.

I had dropped the acid just before sunset, wanting to get the impact of the music and the lightshow of the final acts on Glastonbury's famous pyramid stage, but nothing happened to me for an age. In the event it wasn't until the music had finished and everyone was stumbling back to the tents that the trip kicked in.

It was certainly very powerful even without the music and lights. I was rooted to the spot as the mass of people moved around me watching their bodies stretch, distort and glow in front of my eyes. I just had to sit down and ride it out where I was in the muddy field as colours danced in front of my eyes and my senses opened out to their extremes.

The scariest moment came when the power pylons in the distance started to spark and began to march towards me. The purple, green, and blue lights emanating from these everyday objects were amazing, but the fact that they were moving towards me was really freaking me out.

I couldn't escape though, paralysed by the trip and by the people still moving around me. The pylons were marching closer and closer, spraying out these colourful sparks and all I could do was watch fascinated and frightened.

How long I sat there in that field I don't know, but eventually the visions faded and I was left staring out alone into the dark. The people had all moved on towards the camp area although there were a few passed out bodies strewn around, together with a vast collection of bottles, cans and other litter.

I gradually got to my unsteady feet and followed the path back to where I thought the tent we were staying in was, although when I eventually found it somehow there was no sign of Rod, but at least I could curl up in the dry and pass out myself.

Rod's first acid experience was just as scary – but not so much for him as for me and the others watching. The trip came on just as unexpectedly and as delayed as mine was to be a month or so later, but this time we were on the Isle of Wight ferry.

Although the trip from the Portsmouth Hard to Ryde harbour is only very short, it proved pretty eventful as Rod seemed intent on flying to the island rather than sailing.

The first sign of trouble came as we were boarding when he decided to climb to the upper level of the boat to get a better launch pad for his flight.

With his arms outstretched for take-off it was all I and the three other lads could do to prevent him from diving into the churning waters below the stern.

Of course Rod was convinced he would just soar higher rather than plunge into the harbour, carried aloft by the rows of psychedelic waves surrounding him. He tried to fight us off, and escaped to try and launch himself off the boat again to the concern of the people all around us who were enjoying the late afternoon sun.

Luckily we managed to persuade him that it would be better to head below to the bar and steady ourselves with a few lagers, the first of a few to be taken that day. Once we had got Rod seated in a corner, hemmed in by the rest of us he became calmer and finished his trip in less scary fashion.

By the time we had docked in Ryde, everyone was a lot more relaxed and ready to find some good bars, beer and entertainment.

Eric, the vegan, was our guide as he was the only member of the party who had visited the Isle of Wight in the past – my junior school trip with my sister over ten years previously having been hardly a benchmark for a student night out.

There were, indeed, a good selection of pubs and bars in Ryde town centre, which was reached by a train from the harbour and we must have sampled quite a few.

The full extent of the pub crawl has passed from my memory, but I remember dancing to some decent music in one bar with a pint in my hand – and probably spilling it everywhere – when suddenly all the lights came on and the DJ declared his work was over as it was closing time.

Watches were consulted. Damn, it was 11pm, in those days the designated pub closing time, but more importantly also well past the time the last ferry back to Portsmouth had departed.

We were all having so much fun no-one had thought about our return journey back.

Never mind, said Rod, now fully back to earth after his acid trip, this is a holiday town, so there must be loads of late night bars and discos where we could while away the hours until the first ferry of the morning.

So you would think, but no. I don't know what Ryde is like now – I have never returned to the Isle of Wight since – but in June 1984 there were no drinking establishments available after hours on a Saturday night to quench a student's thirst.

Indeed after 11pm, there was very little open at all in the town, aside from a lone fish & chip shop at which we managed to secure the last scrapings of chips out of the fat fryer.

Taking these, the only food we had eaten nearly all day, we found a bench and a shelter facing the sea in which to contemplate our next move. The major problem, even aside from the lack of bars, clubs and alcohol was the fact that it was turning rather cold, especially with the breeze blowing in off the Solent, and we were all only dressed in t-shirts.

Shivering in this shelter was not doing us any good at all, but there were few other places to go, with the town now deserted and everywhere closed up.

Someone had the great idea of collecting some wood and starting a fire in the shelter to try and keep us warm – it's amazing what sounds sensible to you when you are drunk and stoned enough.

Unfortunately, the only wood they found was a little white picket fence which surrounded the town bowling green.

Nevertheless these were pulled up, broken into pieces and arranged on the floor of the shelter. Five cigarette lighters were eventually emptied trying to light this pile of fencing, which was far from combustible at first, not helped by the wind blowing in from the beach.

Eventually the wood did catch light, but also so did the paint on the fence posts, and this culminated in a vast quantity of black, toxic smoke rather than any actual heat which all blew back towards the bench where we were sitting, sending five choking students scampering out of the shelter, coughing and spluttering.

That scampering soon turned into a flight as the billowing smoke drew the attention of a police patrol car which had been circling the town, with the lights and sirens driving us away from the only shelter and back into the town.

As we paused to draw our breaths, with the police car's sirens fading into the distance, someone decided that the only real option to us was to head back to Ryde railway station and await the first train down to the harbour in the morning.

It was agreed that this was a good idea, and shivering with the cold and still coughing from the smoke and the running we eventually found the town station and managed to gain entrance to the platform.

There were benches there to sit or sleep on, but it was still very cold as we huddled there in just our t-shirts, with at least four hours of night still ahead of us.

But then Rod, who had been exploring further up the platform suggested a solution to the cold benches. He pointed out a large, empty cardboard box propped up against the wall.

This box looked like the sort a big fridge-freezer would have come in, being around eight foot tall and a few feet wide. It was sturdy and with its end-flaps still intact could be made quite secure and, most importantly, wind-proof.

Rod's idea was that the five of us bed down together in this big box – three one end, two the opposite one – which would provide us with everyone's bodily warmth to help stave off hypothermia.

Despite some misgivings, not least due to worries over the body odours and farts which could suffocate us in the box, everyone agreed it would be a neat solution to our predicament.

After a little arguing over who would be sleeping with who and at what end, it was decided that the two biggest guys – Rod and I - would take the north end and the other three the opposite one.

Once we were all settled, with the flaps drawn down to keep out the wind it was all fairly snug within our cardboard world.

It reminded me of the times when, as a child, the arrival of a big box would provide endless fun and excitement. It wasn't what was inside, but what the empty container could be turned into, such as a castle or a rocketship, or whatever the imagination decided.

Of course the stone floor beneath the platform box was hard and unforgiving. But as an ex-Boy Scout I was use to sleeping on the ground, and the warmth generated by our five bodies was very welcome, even with the odd fart and general bodily smells.

Gradually, under the influence of the alcohol, drugs, and other substances taken throughout the day, sleep came to all within the box.

I was probably among the last to drop off, slightly disturbed by Rod's snoring beside me, something I hadn't quite got used to in the six months we had been bunking together, but eventually I too must have passed out. How long the sleep lasted I can't say, but I awoke sometime later to the sounds of movement outside the cardboard walls.

Someone was whistling and there was a scrapping sound which was getting closer and closer to the box. I could feel the others stirring as well although no-one within the container made any noise.

Eventually the scrapping sound came very close to where my head was lying within the box and stopped. I could then hear footsteps around me and suddenly there was a dull thud as someone gave our cardboard container a gentle kick.

I would have loved to have been a fly-on-the-wall watching what happened next, because it certainly must have been a bit of a shock for the kicker.

Almost in a co-ordinated fashion, five heads shot out of each end of the big cardboard box to look enquiringly at what turned out to be a station worker, who had been sweeping the platform floor ahead of the first passengers of the day.

His face was a picture as he could hardly have anticipated the scene, but before he could get a chance to shout 'Platform tickets', the five of us had shot out of the box in opposite directions trying to make for the station exit.

The railway worker stood rooted to the spot, broom in hand, gawping at us, although when the three who had set off in the wrong direction had to turn around and run back past him, he did try to apprehend one of them.

Luckily his actions were to no avail, and all three made it back down the platform and out of the station exit to where Rod and I were awaiting shaking with laughter.

The station cleaner soon appeared at the exit himself but by then we had all scarpered round the corner out of his sight, with the two of us trying to control our mirth, and the other three catching their breath.

If only I could have had a snapshot of that moment the five heads emerging from the cardboard box, and the look on the man's face – it would have been priceless.

The rest of that morning, for by that time it was approaching 6am, passed by fairly peacefully. We had the good fortune to find a cafe quite close to the station open at that time, so retreated in there for big mugs of tea and bacon sandwiches.

After heading back to the station around 7am, and making sure the coast was clear, we hopped a train down to the harbour without being seen by any station staff, and – a major result – managed to persuade the ferry people that we could still use our return tickets back to Portsmouth without having to pay any more money.

I guess they took pity on five poor students, still shivering in their t-shirts even though the sun had by now come up, who must have looked pretty creased, crumpled and sleep-deprived.

Little did they know the secret of the big, brown cardboard box!

Chapter 7: Picnic Table Issues

The picnic table came into our lives during the dog days of our first summer at Clarence Parade.

How it was actually transported there; who made the decision to take it; and why, remained swathed in mystery.

All I really knew is that it is was suddenly there, in the hallway, down the steps from the front door, and it was massive.

Anyone entering the flat would have to edge around the monstrosity, or walk over the top, and it was lucky that the doors to the kitchen and the bathroom both opened inwards or else they could never have been opened!

It was big, solid and wooden – at least eight foot long and four foot or so wide - made to seat up to four people each side on the benches which were bolted to the table's frame.

The planking seemed as big as railway sleepers and it was nearly as heavy – not that I had ever carried a railway sleeper!

Suffice to say, once it had been carried in to Clarence Parade there was really no way it was going to get carried out again.

We knew where it had come from, it was fairly obvious to everyone who stumbled in to it, given that there were six similar ones sitting outside 'The Jolly Sailor' pub at the end of the Parade. That is there were six of them, for now there was a gaping hole where one of them was missing.

What drove the team of people that removed the table from outside the pub – and there must have been at least four of them to carry the thing the 400 yards or so along the road and into our flat – was lost in the annals of time.

We always blamed Rod as he was the ring leader of most of the nefarious activities that occurred at CP. But it could equally have been Jamie or Jan, two of the other fluid inhabitants of the basement flat.

But it was no good blaming anyone. All I knew was that I woke up one Sunday morning in my room at the back of the building, with the hot and cold running damp, went into the hallway to go and use the bathroom, and there it was, blocking my way.

I, of course, cursed and shouted at the table and anyone else who might have heard me at this late part of a Sunday morning, but of course there was no response.

And when I looked into the lounge to see whether any of the culprits were still around, while there were some bodies strewn around the room still sleeping off the effects of the night before, none of them stirred.

I was left to go back into the hallway scratching my head, and managed to edge my way around the table and enter the bathroom to take a shower.

It was always best to get up relatively early if you wanted to take a shower at CP, given that at any one time there could be between five and eight people sleeping there.

It was also always pretty hit and miss if there was hot water anyway, given that the electricity meter needed feeding pretty regularly, and finding enough 50p coins was always an issue.

Mind you that was still a 1,000% improvement on the first flat Rod and I had shared in the final term of our first year at Portsmouth Poly. The place that had left my mother in tears when she and my father had come down to visit and bring some things for their son's first 'home of his own'!

I'm not sure what upset her most – the small size of the one-room bedsit Rod and I shared; the paucity of heating or cooking appliances; the slightly derelict toilet down the hall; or the lack of any bathroom, which meant we had to go and shower at the local Poly Halls of Residence, where thankfully some of our friends were staying! But it was so cheap!!!

The lack of many electrical appliances was actually a very good thing as the flat on Shaftesbury Road – just a few streets back from the Western Common – only had an electricity meter that took 5p coins, which were even harder than 50p's to amass after a night's drinking, and lasted little longer than it took to boil a kettle.

Frequently Rod and I would wake in our small single beds either side of the small basement room - mine was under the street window which I loved, as the postman would often stick any letters through the louvre windows and they would land on me (I have always loved getting post, and letters being delivered onto my bed was a wonderful treat) – gasping for a cuppa, but find the meter had run out during the night and we had no 5p coins to feed it.

Luckily we kept very little in the small fridge, though the pint of milk necessary for our early morning cup of tea would invariably have gone a little rancid if the electricity ran out overnight, so that normally we would have to go out and buy one first thing from the local newsagents – and then ask for all the change in 5p coins, or as much as they had.

Rod and I only stayed in the flat on Shaftesbury Road for a few months before we persuaded our landlord, Mr Fin – not his real name, we think, as he liked to call himself a 'property shark', although cheques were written out to him in that name – that we could take on a bigger flat for the summer.

That property was Clarence Parade, another of Fin's slum-type dwellings, being a big, old, Edwardian property of four or five stories, facing onto the main Southsea Common with a view of the Isle of Wight, the Solent and all the ships passing through it.

CP had been mostly destroyed by a fire earlier in the year and lacked most of its roof, with the only habitable part of the building the basement flat we were offered – again at a knock-down rate.

Although the floors above were mostly gutted, the basement was pretty sturdy, with four bedrooms, a big lounge, a bathroom, a kitchen and the now blocked hallway.

It suited us because we could halve the rent by getting two other cost-conscience students in as well – including my old Southsea digs mate Richard 'Mad Guitar' Axton, and an otherwise motley assortment of Rod's friends and party comrades. There was also plenty of room in the lounge for other transients.

Once we had got the TV and video package organised – although Radio Rentals were a little loathe to install at the address – we were sorted for a pleasant, almost homely abode.

But right now that homeliness was under threat from the blasted picnic table in the hall.

At first it was a bit of a laugh and a good story to tell, with people popping round to view the said table and everyone in CP getting fairly used to traversing the item on their way in and out of the flat.

But after the first month it got to be a bit of a nuisance and we started to investigate ways of removing the offending object. Taking it apart was one option, as there was no way we could lift it back out of the flat. However, all our limited supply of tools and implements could not cope with the big bolts, tightened up to industrial strength, necessary to remove the benches and the legs.

We had just about given up on the idea and resigned ourselves to life with the picnic table until one Sunday afternoon in September bought a knock at the door.

It was around lunchtime, and most of the occupants of the flat were still sleeping off the previous night's drink and drugs hangover, but I was up so I went to answer the door.

I opened it wide at first and then, almost instantly shut it back to a crack so that no one could see the picnic table planted in the hall, because standing there were two uniformed police officers.

Now given that my father was a constable in the Metropolitan Police for thirty years I was fairly use to the sight of the constabulary, and normally quiet relaxed in their presence. But now, given the looming presence of the stolen picnic table and the all-pervading smell of weed which always emanated from the flat, I was perhaps understandably taken aback by their surprise presence outside the door of Clarence Parade.

I stammered out a 'good afternoon' to the two officers as the nearest one to me tried to peer around the door.

"Errr, what can we do for you, officers?" I continued, in a cautious tone, making sure the constable could not see around behind me.

"Does Rod Constanti live here?" replied the officer next to him.

"Why?", I quickly countered, swerving the confirmation of my friend's presence in the flat or not.

"We'd just like to talk to him," the policeman continued. "Is he here?"

"No", I lied, not knowing what Rod could have been up to that required the presence of the police, and unwilling to admit that he was in the flat.

"But does he actually live here?", the officer asked again.

I must have a look a little furtive and confused as I weighed up my answer, so the policeman who had been trying to peer behind the door, chimed in: "Could we come in, please?"

"No!", I said, rather abruptly as I tried to close the door even more in front of me, almost just leaving my head poking out.

"Is that 'No' he does not live here?" continued the first constable.

At that moment I heard a noise behind me and looked around to see that someone had emerged from the lounge and was climbing over the picnic table headed for the bathroom. Luckily in their druggie stupor they were far from aware of me at the door, let alone the two police officers I was talking too, otherwise paranoia could have got the better of them.

I turned back as the policeman questioned me again.

"All we want to know is if Rod lives here? He hasn't done anything bad, we just have a message for him."

I ran through in my mind all the messages that a policeman could want to give to Rod, and all of them were bad. I thought back to the time, almost a year earlier, when I had been called out of a history lecture by the senior member of staff to be told that I should call my mother as my dad had been in an accident.

I panicked then, having lived through various scenarios where my father could have been killed or injured in his police career, having been involved as a firearms trained officer at some of the important events of the 70's including the Balcombe Street siege, where IRA members had barricaded themselves into a house with hostages, and being present when bombs had been exploded by the Irish terrorists, notably at the London Boat Show.

He had moved away from the more dangerous assignments he carried out with the Special Patrol Group a few years earlier to take up a more sedentary position as a policeman on the Carriage Gates outside the Palace of Westminster, which was a relief to my mum.

Although at the end of his first week guarding Parliament, Mrs Thatcher's former Northern Ireland minister, Airey Neave was blown-up by a car bomb as he was driving out of the underground car park just yards away from where my dad was standing, which didn't help her nerves.

Anyway, at least this time it was only a motorcycle accident on his daily commute. He was actually fairly close to home when a car pulled out of a turning in front of him and his Honda C90 had smacked into the side of it, sending him barrelling over the bonnet and landing him on the tarmac, luckily with no other cars coming in the opposite direction.

He had smashed up his knee pretty badly, and was bruised all over but thankfully sustained no lasting injuries, although he gave up motorbiking from then on and only drove his car in to work.

Luckily as well, because he was close to home, he got taken to the local Bromley hospital, making it easier for my mother and sister to go to visit him as he recovered from his injuries.

I travelled home as soon as I heard of the accident, to see that he was alright, with the dispensation of the senior lecturer, which was also a good cure for the slight home sickness I had been starting to feel. I stayed the weekend and soon cured myself of that, having found I had actually got use to having my own space and doing my own thing.

Anyway, hearing the policeman talk of a message for Rod bought back the memories and made me worry at what might have happened to his family. I knew that his mother was divorced, and he had no siblings, but anything could have happened to bring the police calling.

"He does live here," I said more confidently. "But he isn't in currently," I added, a bear-faced lie given that I had seen him pass out on his bed about eight hours previously.

"Can I take the message for him?" I asked, hoping not to sound too desperate, and wishing that the officers would just go away.

The one nearest the door crack was still looking suspiciously at me and clearly wanted to see inside the otherwise derelict building.

His colleague was more affable, however, and said my suggestion would be fine.

"It's nothing major," he added. "Just ask him to call his mum. There is nothing wrong, it is just that she hasn't heard from him for almost 8 weeks and is getting worried."

The worry drained out of me, but any relief from the news that nobody in Rod's family had died or been injured, was replaced by a slight anger that my friend's insensitivity to the worries of his mother had almost called down a full-scale police raid on CP!

I mumbled a 'Thanks' and shut the door on the two coppers. I remained standing on the step collecting my thoughts and saw that their two helmets were still visible through the skylight above the door. But eventually I saw that they had moved off and as, breathing a sigh of relief, I turned back to descend the three stone steps and traverse the offending picnic table, I heard the toilet flush go.

A moment later the bolt was slid back on the bathroom door, it was opened and out emerged Rod.

I had been too distracted to see that it was him going into the room earlier, but as he came out he called to me in a fairly stoned sounding voice: "What you doing, man?"

We were both separated by the table that dominated the hallway so even if I had been tempted to take hold off his throat and give it a good shake for helping scare the life out of me, I was prevented from doing so by eight foot of distressed pine.

I controlled myself, and responded in fairly measured tones: "I was just answering a knock at the door."

"Hey man, who was it? The dealerman – we need some more weed?"

I glowered at his innocence, being aware of how close we could have come to being banged up for possession of said weed by our recently departed visitors.

"No, quite the opposite. It was the police!", I answered. Letting the word hang precipitously in the air.

Rod looked shocked, and clutched his always too small for him silk dressing gown close to his body.

"Shit! What did they want? They didn't see anything? Smell anything? You didn't let them in, did you?", stammered my friend in a staccato line of questions.

I glared back him. "Of course not!", I said indignantly. "They wanted to see you?"

"What?!", gabbered my friend. "Why? I ain't don't nothing. The picnic table … drugs … student protests. Nothing!"

I was tempted to string him along and claim they wanted him to go down to the station and help them with their enquiries, but I was too kind and simply told him the truth.

"It was your mother. She sent them. She is worried about you. Says you haven't called her for two months, so she called the police to see if you are still alive!"

"Jesus!", Rod responded, obviously slightly relieved. "What the fuck!"

"Indeed! You had better call her and get the cops off our backs," I said, rather sanctimoniously. "And we'd better find a way to get rid of this bloody picnic table, in case they come back before then."

Rod nodded his head vigorously: "Absolutely. I'll put Little Ron on it. He must know a way of getting this thing apart."

In a gesture of contempt, he kicked out at the bench that was in front of him, a foolish move given that he only had some flimsy slippers on.

There was a yelp of pain. I couldn't help but smile. Although Rod was a good mate, he couldn't half be a twat at times.

But he was as good as his word. And within days of the unexpected police visit, Little Ron had indeed driven round in his Ford Capri, with a box of tools and helped us dismantle the beast in the hall.

Little Ron was an acquaintance of Rod's from east London, who was a student on some vocational course and lived in the north of Portsmouth, hence we didn't see too much of him. But given that he had the luxury of a car, he was the go-to-guy in any tricky situations.

Even after we had dismantled the picnic table, we were still left with a pile of planks and the table top to dispose of, and there was no way it was all going to fit in the Capri.

We would have to wait until the dead of night and sneak out with the bits, dumping them somewhere on Portsmouth Common. That was, of course, more than a two man job and involved some planning to ensure that we didn't just get completely stoned and forget about it.

So, finally, over the course of a few nights, two of us would steal out of the flat after midnight carrying a few planks and abandon them in different places around the common before scarpering back.

The actual table top took more of us to shift, around four, and a bit more thought. It was hard enough to negotiate it out of the hall, up the stone steps and out of the door, but then we had to find a place to dump the offending item.

Luckily, a few doors down from CP some builders had recently had a skip delivered so we were able to manhandle the slab of pine on top of that, and run off very quickly.

And then it was gone. We had our flat back. The hallway was clear, we could freely enter the bathroom, and any visiting police officers would not be arresting us for theft - just for the copious amount of drugs that littered the premises!

Rod phoned his mother and placated her and we never saw the rozzers again at CP. Life could continue on as normal.

Chapter 7: Party Politics

Every day could be party time at Clarence Parade given the ever-changing occupants of the burnt-out building.

Although Rod, 'Mad Guitar' Axton and myself were the constants in the basement flat over the nine months or so we lived there, various other students took up residence in the other bedroom and often on the sofa at the property.

Given Rod's involvement with the Militant Tendency during this time – Portsmouth Poly elected a Militant supporter as NUS president in our final year – many meetings were held in CP and these would often degenerate into a smoking and drinking fest.

As a result, many of the Militant guys – and they all were male – would crash at the flat, with some staying for a matter of weeks at a time, including Dave, the future NUS president.

There was no membership of the tendency given that it was an interventionist Trotskyite movement within the Labour Party, which supported a fortnightly paper. But during the divisive coal miners strike which dominated the early year's of Margaret Thatcher's reign as she battled to smash the power of the unions, Militant held some influence as Labour struggled to come to terms with the Conservative government's policies.

Derek Hatton's election as mayor in Liverpool during the period was the zenith of the tendency's power within the party, but having the only Militant NUS president was a big boost to the supporters at Portsmouth Poly.

I myself never really put my backing behind Militant, though I did occasionally help Rod with paper sales outside the Student's Union as well as to workers around the Portsmouth Dockyards. I was a member of the Labour Party having been indoctrinated by the Marxist influences of the historical studies course at the polytechnic. A number of our lecturers – who included some Oxbridge alumni – were activists in the party, and the options I took such as Revolutions in France and British Labour History reflected my political interests.

But although I was definitely anti-Thatcher and the Conservatives and prepared to march, picket and vote against her government's policies, I thought that this could be achieved through membership of Labour, and didn't like the Militant campaign to undermine the party leadership, however ineffectual they seemed.

I remained a Labour party member throughout the 1980's and for most of the 1990's until I resigned after the election of Tony Blair as leader. My view was that New Labour was fair removed from my socialist roots and no longer represented my views – which of course was fairly ironic given their election successes and dominance of politics in the UK for the following decade.

However, I think my break with the party also reflected some inconsistencies in those socialist views given that by that time I was working as a financial journalist, reporting on the UK stock market, and living in a mortgaged-house in the London suburbs with my Conservative-supporting wife.

Really my political views were far from strongly held, and the Marxist indoctrination at Portsmouth, while introducing me to some great historians and writers, only had a limited impact. Other of my classmates managed to maintain their independent views, not least the one I still continue to have the most contact with - 'Fascist' Mark. He is actually one of only two Historical Studies classmates I keep in contact with, although I do have regular meetings with a number of other Portsmouth Poly graduates, all from the drama group of which I was a member.

Indeed, it was a recent meet-up with that group of friends from Polydrama that prompted me to scribble down these Portsmouth memories, given that they seem never to tire of my telling them some of the stories that I have included in this tome.

I had long been bitten by the acting bug having started in primary school where I remember playing Simple Simon the Pieman – was it because I was slightly obese!

By the final year at Alexandra Junior School in Sydenham I had co-written and starred in the end of term production with my best-mate Johnnie Allen. I remember we thought it hilarious to do some sketches as The Two Johnnies, a take-off of the Two Ronnies TV comedy show at the time – obviously we missed the irony of the name!

That was of course, the height of my acting career (unless you count my failed audition to be TV's 'Just William' at 10 – I could have been the next Dennis Waterman!), for although I appeared in a vast number of productions in senior school, and even did a Theatre Arts A/O level in the sixth form, I would never have a leading role again.

Unless, of course, you count playing the Evil Queen in Snow White, my final pantomime for Polydrama. That was wonderful fun – squeezing into my then girlfriend's high heels which I had to kick off whenever I exited the stage;

'singing' Gloria Gaynor's disco classic 'I Will Survive'; and of course just wearing a wig and a dress!

By then I was president of the drama society, so could dictate the roles I wanted to play, but to be honest I really could only play myself and was never very good at that.

My favourite role, however, came after I had graduated from Portsmouth having remained in the city and found work and a flat with the same girlfriend who had lent me the high heels – and would shortly afterwards become my wife.

I was allowed to remain a member of Polydrama after graduating and was cast as Tom, the Rambling Vet in a brilliant production of 'Table Manners' – the first part of Alan Ayckbourne's wonderful 'Norman Conquests' trilogy.

That was a joyous role in a great play with a perfect cast, which had my good friend – and now a former BBC reporter – Tim Jenkins as the eponymous Norman. And it was the last time I ever trod the boards having realised how one-dimensional my acting was, and – more importantly – how bad my memory was for learning lines.

I'm not sure I really miss it nearly 30 years on, for to be honest it was the social aspect of Polydrama that I most enjoyed – making new friends, not on the same course who had a love for theatre in common and having summer picnics and parties, including the ubiquitous post-production festivities.

And it was one of those post-production parties that most sticks out in my memory of the times at Clarence Parade.

It was actually after the first pantomime we had done at Polydrama while I was there – a production of 'Aladdin' –

which was my second show with the group, having played a clergyman in 'The Happiest Days of our Lives' in my second term down in Portsmouth.

Aladdin was put on in the December of my second year, just before the end of term, and given its big cast and crew warranted a more substantial party than the post-pub celebrations normally undertaken, so I volunteered the use of my room in CP.

I had two minor roles in the pantomime, playing the Grand Vizier, and at the end – for some strange reason – a Mummy! This involved me wearing a balaclava hat and being wrapped in bandages by the attractive stage manager, Lindsey – the girl who would later become my wife.

Pictures from the production show that it was fairly hard to keep all the bandages in place around my body, with the black balaclava definitely showing through, but Lindsey did her best, and we certainly bonded over the role.

It was at the after-cast party for Aladdin that we really hit it off, much to the chagrin of a number of the other cast members – who are still my friends – who had taken a shine to her.

But – apologies to my now ex-wife - the party was more memorable for an amazing piece of impersonation by one of the younger cast members, and a brilliant wind-up that it generated.

Russell was the out-and-out star of Aladdin, his first production for Polydrama, playing the Genie with comic skill and panache. Every one of his lines drew a laugh and he easily outshone the lovely Tina, who played Aladdin and the rest of the cast.

Not only was Russell a very funny actor, he was also a brilliant mimic and raconteur off-stage. He was at his very best when doing his Rowan Atkinson skits, and was an excellent Blackadder or Mr Bean. It helped that he bore a physical resemblance to the superstar comedian, being of slight build and dark-haired.

And it was at the post-Aladdin party that we really first saw all his skills, although we rather cruelly used it to given him a slight knock-back.

The drink was flowing, some weed was being smoked and my fairly large bedroom at CP – with its hot-and-cold running damp, interesting collection of fungi spores, and view of the burnt-out back of the property – was pretty full, with around a dozen people still left at the party after midnight.

Russell was sitting at the back of the room on the slightly mouldy, and very off-white sofa that took up most of the area under the single-glazed window. He was surrounded by around four or five people, with Lindsey sitting next to him on the sofa.

He was just getting in to the flow of what we came to know as his party piece – a take-off of a Rowan Atkinson 'Mr Angry' sketch ('And another thing, what about the bloody trains …' etc). The consummate comedian was ad-libbing it, taking cues from those around him to riff on and everyone was laughing heartily.

One of those watching was a Liverpudlian student who had had a minor role in the pantomime but who was always fairly quiet and self-effacing. His name was Mike Groves, and his Dad was slightly famous – being a member of folk group 'The Spinners', who everyone remembered from countless TV programmes in the 70's, wearing Arran sweaters and singing Irish airs.

Mike was pretty shy and rarely bought up his Dad's fame, even when 'The Spinners' played the Portsmouth Guildhall later that same year.

But one wag – it wasn't me, honest! - decided that it would be a good idea to feed Russell 'The Spinners' as a subject for him to be Mr Angry about. It worked like a dream …

"The Bloody Spinners, don't get me started about the bloody Spinners…." And he was away.

He ranted on about their bloody Arran jumpers, the quality of their singing, the time wasted on British TV showing their boring performances … he was easily going on for nearly five minutes with his vociferous attack on the UK folk legends.

All the time everyone around him were laughing until they split, with other people looking over to see what was causing the intense jollity. Of course, they all knew what Russell didn't – about Mike Groves' Dad's role in 'The Spinners'.

Mike was simply leaning against the wall, quietly smiling to himself, and occasionally laughing – because he would have been among the first to acknowledge that 'The Spinners' were hardly a top-draw for the UK music world.

Russell was still in his flow, however, when Lindsey gently intervened with the killer line: "By the way Russell, do you know who Mike's Dad is?"

This stopped the rant in mid-air, while Russell turned to look at the urbane young man to his left – who actually was wearing an Arran jumper (I swear!)

And then Lindsey delivered the punch-line: "He is one of the singers in 'The Spinners'!"

The room exploded into laughter, led by Mike Groves himself, as Russell's comedic balloon was well and truly burst.

The erstwhile mimic looked extremely crestfallen and immediately started apologising profusely to Mike for having made his father the butt of a very large joke.

But Mike was, of course, far from upset by Russell's monologue and found it all very funny, although not as funny as the opportunity had been to take the pantomime star down a peg or two.

We of course all felt very cruel, and also apologised ourselves to Russell for having wound him up so completely, although the laughter was still ringing too.

The party continued, everyone had a good time and the slight embarrassment was soon completely forgotten.

Russell went on to be the stalwart of many Polydrama productions, not least pantomimes, writing and performing sketches for Rag Week, even scripting and starring in the long lost Polydrama James Bond movie – never completed or viewed as far as I know.

He continued to keep us all entertained with his spot-on Rowan Atkinson impersonations and generally was the life and soul of every party or event.

I think he has forgiven us all for the wind-up, and I hope he forgives me for scribbling down this story of his slightly embarrassing debut, for he is a wonderful friend and drinking companion still.

There were, of course, other parties at Clarence Parade, but none of them as raucous and such good fun as that first Polydrama one, mainly – perhaps – because I remember it the best as I wasn't completely pissed or stoned out of my skull.

Chapter 8: Common View

Life at Clarence Parade didn't actually last that long. It was no surprise given the state of the property above our basement but Mr Finn indicated we needed to move out after the summer term of our second year, so we were only in the flat for less than a year.

It was certainly a landmark - just find the ruined building facing Southsea Common and the Solent – but given that clear run across the grass, the shingle beach and out towards the English Channel winter in the basement was pretty cold and inhospitable.

There was frost on the inside of windows; wind whistling through all the cracks; the ubiquitous hot and cold running damp; and any number of infestations to make CP life interesting.

Indeed life at a seaside resort – for Southsea was still that - was always pretty dismal outside of the summer. Most of the entertainments, cafes, chippies, and the like were all shut for around six months of the year, so there was always a deserted feel to the seafront and Common, which together with the weather gave everything a rather desolate look.

Of course it is always better to look back at the time in Clarence Parade through the rose-coloured glasses engendered by the copious amounts of drugs, alcohol, and jollity we had there, but there was still another year of studying to go, a summer on the dole to survive, and a new flat to find.

In the end, Rod and I were the only two CP occupants to stay together after we had to move out, but now there was an added complication in that Rod had a permanent girlfriend – Amanda - who would be moving in as well.

We wanted to stay in Southsea, close to the Common and therefore the lecture rooms, library, Student's Union and friendly pubs. In fact we found somewhere quite close to where Rod and I first shared a gloomy bedsit, right on the Common again, but this time facing away from the sea, and across the dog-leg towards the dockyards on Western Parade.

We were no longer in a basement either, having a second floor flat with an almost-balcony where you could perch with your feet dangling down and admire the view, which normally involved a few football matches taking place on the more sheltered side of the common.

It was a long and narrow flat with a lounge/bedroom – which I occupied – at the front encompassing the almost-balcony; a small single bedroom to its side also with a view over the Common; a corridor where the main entrance was which led down some steps to a fairly large kitchen and carried on down past the bathroom to a big double bedroom at the back – which Rod and Mandy occupied.

The occupant of the single bedroom changed a number of times over the year or so we lived there, being friends of Rod or Mandy and therefore invariably either vegan or vegetarian, Millitant or Socialist Worker.

Many meetings were held of various groupings in my lounge/bedroom which was never ideal, particularly when it was getting to essay deadlines and exam revision for my final year, so there were a few raised words at times and things became a little strained with Rod.

To be honest, most of the time I was spending the evenings and weekends with a different group of friends – the Polydrama players mainly – and seeing Lindsey, who was by then my permanent girlfriend. But every so often things would boil over as Mandy – a large, fiery, red-head – coaxed Rod into saying something about how I needed to share my space more with other people.

I couldn't really be bothered to argue, although the times I did come back from the pub and find the two of them and their friends smoking on the sofa and watching the telly I thought I was normally fairly affable, making them tea before crashing out at the far end of the room.

The couple also spent most of their time together in their far bedroom anyway, which had it's own small TV and Rod was in such thrall to his girlfriend there was little real social interaction anymore.

Mealtimes could be a social occasion, however, and Mandy – who was on the same history course as Rod and I but had not really been among our circle much before – would make very delicious and tasty vegan casseroles, chillis and curries.

I was very happy to be largely vegetarian myself at this time, not through any altruism or political reasoning, but because it was much cheaper to eat that way, especially when we were all sharing!

However, I could not completely given up all meat, and there was one area which would prove to be a flashpoint – bacon!

I was allocated one shelf to myself in the communal fridge so that any meat products I might buy would not contaminate anywhere else, and it would normally just accommodate some eggs, butter, and the afore-mentioned bacon to provide an occasional fry-up when the hang-over needed some proper fuel.

That wasn't very often. I was finding that I was drinking less than I had been with my new group of friends, smoking less weed, and taking fewer other drugs, although there were still plenty of evenings when all the components would come together and the frying pan would be the first thing I thought of when I came to in the morning. Then I would creep down to the kitchen, open all the windows – to neutralise the obnoxious smells – and reach for the bacon in the fridge …

However, as was becoming increasingly more frequent, the smoky, lovely rashers were not always there. They had gone. Been stolen, eaten by someone else. But who could do such a thing??!! Everyone else in the flat was a professed vegetarian, if not vegan, and was foresworn any of the piggy products. Could someone from outside have pilfered the packet of porky goodness? Or was one of the vegetarians really a wolf in sheep's clothing?! I had my suspicions.

Those grew when one afternoon – having had an unsatisfying breakfast of just fried eggs and fried bread – I returned to the fridge for some milk to add to my cup of tea and found that a fresh packet of bacon had materialised on my shelf.

Given that no one else had entered the flat that day, but I had seen and heard Rod go out briefly and return from the shops, my suspicions looked to have been confirmed. I didn't want to confront him in front of rabid vegan Mandy about his bacon pinching, so it was hard to get my friend on his own to question about what he had done with the original bacon. I, of course, assumed he must have eaten it – but when and how without arousing Mandy's suspicions was the burning question.

Eventually, Mandy had to go out somewhere by herself, and Rod and I were left alone over a cup of tea and a large reefer, giving me the opportunity to raise the pork pilfering.

"I know you stole my bacon," I launched in, "which is fine – and thanks for putting some back – but how on earth and when did you get to eat it all?"

Rod looked sheepish – obviously no longer a wolf – and apologised for the larceny.

"I was desperate," he added. "It is tough trying to be vegan, and the one thing that really makes it difficult is the thought of that bacon. Frying in the pan, sizzling away, the smell of that smoked goodness, the little bits caramelised in the pan that you can scrape up and eat … it's like food porn!"

I laughed, completely understanding his dilemma, although I always had the get-out clause that I was only a social vegetarian!

"I had to have it," Rod continued. "I even bunked off a Labour history seminar to come back to the flat and cook up the bacon when I knew no one would be about, and Mandy would be at her Witchcraft lecture."

There was something ironic about Rod, the Labour activist having to miss his favourite course to defy the Witch Mandy and hog out on bacon!

"You must have been very desperate," I said. "Did Mandy not suspect anything?"

"I cooked up the whole packet, and stuffed it all into one sandwich, with loads of ketchup," my friend answered. "I gobbled it down – it was so delicious."

"I then washed everything up straight away" – an unheard of act in a student flat where washing up could languish for days – "and went down the pub to have few pints to try and get the bacon taste and smell out of my mouth," Rod confessed. "And when I met up with Mandy later I took her to the smokiest, smelliest pub and then out for a curry after – insisting on having a vegetable Phall!"

"If all that didn't neutralise the bacon smell I don't know what would have done. It also meant she didn't really want to come anywhere near me all night!," he concluded.

"I bet you still suffered for all that after though?", I said.

"In more ways than one," my friend added. "Aside from a horrendous time on the toilet, which could have been the not being used to eating meat, the ten pints of lager, or the curry – Mandy was still not speaking to me for much of the next day!"

I stopped myself from replying that I would have found that last bit to be a very pleasant consequence, for I knew Rod was very aware that my feelings for his girlfriend were not as warm as his own.

"Oh well, no harm done," I said, instead, lamely. "You know you can always steal any bacon whenever you like, but I'll try not to keep to many temptations in the fridge for you."

"Thanks mate," Rod replied. "I'd appreciate that. Mandy is far from comfortable about having 'dead animal' in her flat anyway, and has moaned to me about it a number of times."

I bit my tongue again. "Her flat!", I wanted to say, "It was always just our flat." But I stopped myself, though I was saddened by how distant how friendship was becoming.

It probably was not being fair to blame it all on Mandy. As I have said my life was moving on too, particularly with Lindsey, although there was certainly never any suggestion that we would move in together - and even when that did happen a year or so on, it remained a secret from her parents for a long while.

But relationships undoubtedly put strains on long-term friendships and although Rod and I would remain good mates throughout our time at Portsmouth, living in the same flats for most of our three year course, when it was all over we almost never saw each again.

He moved back to East London – with Mandy – and I hope settled down, married, had kids, found a good job and is living happily ever after.

I stayed in Portsmouth after graduating in June 1986 because Lindsey – who had finished the year before – had decided to remain in Southsea then and found a job in the city and settled in a flat-share with another girl.

I too found a job fairly soon after finishing, albeit drawing on my year's work experience at the Greenwich Building Society before I had started at Portsmouth Poly rather than my 2:1 Historical Studies degree, becoming a mortgage broker.

Perhaps, given that Lindsey and I had met through the drama group, it was no surprise that the friends we kept in contact with mostly came from Polydrama, and over thirty years on that is mostly still the case – even though Lindsey and I got married and divorced within the first ten years.

There are still two guys from the Historical Studies course that I do keep in fairly close contact with – 'Fascist' Mark and Manfred – but mostly because they are both London-based and it is easier to keep up the ties.

Rod, however, could still live in London, but I completely lost contact with him never even having had his mother's address.

In this age of social media it would, perhaps be fairly easy to have a search for him, but would it be right. We shared a lot together in Portsmouth – most of it fuelled by drugs and alcohol – but it would be impossible to recreate any of the magic, and is probably best to leave it at that.

I was prompted a few years back to think of Rod again when I was introduced to former West Ham footballer, Tony Cottee by a business acquaintance.

I remembered that my Portsmouth friend had been a fervent Irons fan, and had mentioned that he had known Cottee – a star player for the club when only a teenager – when he was growing up. But I thought it a little tenuous to ask this fairly famous footballer whether he had ever known a Rod Constanti when growing up in East London, so I let the moment pass.

He might have said "never heard of him" and that would have tarnished the magic.

Chapter 9: Game On

As I have mentioned, my life in Portsmouth did not end after my graduation from the polytechnic and I remained in the city for almost another 18 months.

I found a room on my own in a flat share on Albany Road well away from the delights of the Common and seafront, nearer the high street, far removed from Clarence Parade and the other abodes Rod and I shared.

My new flat mates were not students, but employed graduates, and I was desperate to get my own job and an income. Lindsey was in her own flat share a short walk away and working for an insurance brokerage just around the corner from where my lectures used to take place in King's Rooms.

That summer after graduation was a fairly lonely time as all my other friends had moved away, back home or to new jobs and cities. I had decided not to run home but stay and show my support for Lindsey who had moved down to be near me a year earlier, but it took a while to find a job and there wasn't much to do, particularly with little money coming in.

One of my lecturers, Ken Lunn, did set me to work doing some research for him in the Poly library which kept me occupied for a while – though I don't remember getting any credit when his book came out!

I even applied to be on a TV gameshow, something I would not have thought of doing before or since, and actually got accepted after an interview in Southampton.

It was for a new ITV production, called 'Runway", which did last longer than the first series I was in – for five seasons overall!

The host was a very nice man called Chris Searle, who had been one of Esther Rantzen's men on the long-running 'That's Life' show on the BBC. He did only last the first series though – before being replaced by Richard Madeley, later of Richard & Judy fame!

Searle's USP was the chunky sweaters which he wore in varying shades and changed for each of his 50 shows, though according to varying reports there was at least one continuity issue where a different jumper appeared in the same show, which had had to be re-shot. This happened because the winning contestant from one show carried over to do his 'Runway' quiz final at the start of the next show – not that I got that far!

It was, however, a great few days of filming up in Manchester at Granada studios. Lindsey came with me and we drove up because the petrol money being paid was superior to the train fare costs, and we got put up in a swanky hotel in the city. Well it looked swanky, and as we found out its guests for the night we were there included both the Kirov Opera company from St Petersburg and all the cyclists from the Round Britain Milk Race.

We only found this out, however, because at 2.30 in the morning one of the drunken Russian guests managed to set off the hotel fire alarm and we all had to de-camp out of the building and stand in the freezing cold in our nightwear while the fire brigade did its checks. Not that the cyclists had changed out of their racing gear, and most were still carrying their expensive bicycles over their shoulders.

Eventually we got back to sleep – although there was still a lot of singing and too-ing and fro-ing by the Russians – before having to get up early in the morning for the car to take us to the hallowed Granada studios.

Hallowed certainly for my paternal grandmother who was a massive fan of 'Coronation Street', and was thrilled when I told her I would be getting a tour of the set. I am afraid though - aside from peaking in when my Gran was watching it in our lounge when she and Pop came up for their annual August holiday to London – it all meant nothing to me nor to Lindsey. But it was nice to see.

Anyway the gameshow filming was quite exciting, with three shows being taped on the same day and although there was a live audience and I knew lots of people could eventually be watching it – even though it had an early morning slot – I was not at all nervous.

However, being confident about being able to answer the questions was one thing, being first to the buzzer to actually get to do that was another! My co-ordination has always been terrible and I was rarely able to get a buzz in first, consequently by the end of the second round I was trailing the other two contestants, and – as the youngest – was looking pretty stupid.

However, all of that was to change in the final knock-out round, even though - because I was in last place - I had no choice over the category of questions I was to be asked and my stone banker of 'British Prime Ministers' was taken by another contestant.

In the end I was landed with 'Japanese phrases', something for which I felt prepared to commit hari-kari over but which in fact turned out to be a triumph for me. I ended up answering nine out of the ten phrases correctly – it must have been all that time watching 'Shogun' with Richard Chamberlain! The only one I got wrong I actually turned in to the only joke made on the show – calling, whatever the phrase was, 'The Art of Bed-Making', and eliciting laughter from the audience and from Chris Searle.

It was not enough to get me into first place, but it had hauled me up to second and spared my blushes. And sitting in the audience after filming had finished to watch the final show recording of the day I actually didn't regret not coming first, as the Runway part of the show was much harder and more nerve-wracking, and I definitely would not have got all the questions right.

As it was I did get a quite expensive, large Delsey plastic suitcase as a prize, plus a unique Runway branded holdall and leather passport cover, and a mug (the only thing I still have) – I had to abandon the suitcase in the loft when I moved house five years ago as having had a ladder fitted after putting it up there it would not fit back through the hole!

We also had a very nice meal that evening with all the other contestants, Chris Searle and the production team, and another night at the posh Manchester hotel – this time without any fire alarm interruptions.

The only slight disappointment was that – despite being promised – Granada TV never notified us of when the show I was in would be broadcast, and given that it was on at 9am in the morning, when most people were at work, no one was going to be able to see it unless it was video recorded.

No-one that is aside from my paternal Grandmother who it turned out watched the show religiously waiting for her grandson to come on and phoned my parents one evening to say how marvellous it was to see me on the telly! I never have seen the show with me in, though I did write to Granada and ask them whether it would be re-broadcast.

I know in this age when there are 100's of TV channels, some even dedicated to the world of gameshows, 'Runway' has been retransmitted a number of times, but I am never going to be dedicated to finding out when the first series is on and recording all 50 episodes just to see the one with me in.

On the internet there are some clips of the show on 'You Tube' and other websites, but I have found no sign of my TV gameshow debut there either.

It is probably for the best, however, I would not like to guess what 80's clothing and hairstyle I might have been sporting. That has certainly been blanked from my memory!

Chapter 10: A Sense of Place

The summer after graduation dragged on. The search for a job, any job was a grind and living on the dole, housing benefit and the fag-end of my credit card was all very stressful.

At least the weather was pleasant, the beach and the sea close by, and I could see Lindsey most evenings after she had finished her work. But it was still quite a lonely existence, with my new flatmates all having jobs, and none of the delights of Clarence Parade life being recreated.

I spent a lot of the time in the polytechnic library reading and scanning the papers for jobs to apply for and general news, and writing countless letters. It was while doing these chores that I hit on the idea of organising a lecture in Portsmouth by my favourite historian, Dr Richard Cobb, then the retired Professor of Modern History at Oxford University.

Cobb's works on the French Revolution of 1789 were the one factor which kept me sane whilst studying the period in my second year at Portsmouth. Our tutor on the Revolutions course, Roger Thomas, was obsessed with his books on the subject, notably, of the 'Police and the People', and it was an easy way of keeping up your grades by including plenty of Cobb quotes in your essays.

It helped that I actually enjoyed reading his prose and understood more of what he was trying to say than that of some of the more Marxist interpretations of the revolutionary period. Cobb managed to straddle the Liberal/Marxist divide by having studied in France alongside the renowned communist historian Albert Soboul, and writing about rank and file revolutionaries rather than the elite – his main work written in French was on the Revolutionary Army.

But aside from his body of historical writings, Cobb had also written some entertaining memoirs, the first of which rung a chord with me as it was about his childhood in Tunbridge Wells in Kent – the town were Lindsey had been bought up as well. Indeed, the book – 'Still Life' – even had a map of Tunbridge Wells in it which I used to navigate around the town when I first went there to visit her!

I hadn't really thought through how and where a lecture by Dr Cobb in Portsmouth would actually take place, but I still wrote him an invite – in effect a fan letter – and mailed it to his publishers address, fully expecting never to get a reply. It was a bit like my application to appear on a quiz show – not something I really thought would happen.

So, imagine my surprise when probably a month or so later a small pale blue envelope dropped on to the mat of my flat-share in Southsea, with a slightly scruffy type-written address.

Inside the envelope, there were three pages of the same coloured paper, typed on a single-side, with the first headed from '165, Godstow Road, Wolvercote, Oxford', and signed at the bottom in blue ink 'Yours ever, Richard Cobb'. By a miracle, the famous historian had replied.

This long, rather rambling letter started off: "I say, I say, I did not think I could have had any fans in YOUR age group, I have had quite a few letters from residents, or former residents of Tunbridge Wells, but most of them have come from the 65 to the 95 age groups, I expect I may still get one or two from those who have topped a century."

The historian, who was then almost 70, went on to reveal that, aside from the Tunbridge Wells connection, he had also spent a lot of time as a child in Southsea, as his mother's sister was married to a Naval doctor and lived at 10, Nettlecombe Avenue – by a weird coincidence the same road in which I had my first Southsea digs.

Cobb also revealed that he had even previously given a talk at Portsmouth Poly some years previously, when the brother of one of his Balliol pupils, Tim Heald was down there.

The letter went on to mention that he remembered being "taken to see Aladdin and that sort of thing on the Pier" and that he "once saw a seaplane that won the Schneider Trophy." Cobb added that: "Being keen on Dickens as a child, Portsmouth was rather a hallowed place." As a Dickens fan myself I had visited the author's birthplace museum in the city many times.

Excitingly, the historian went on to say that he must come down to see me there, noting that he had an OAP Railcard and that there was a direct train from Oxford so it "would be quite an easy day trip".

He added that some time in October would be best for him – as he and his 45-year-old wife were about to go on their annual holiday to Whitby – and commented: "Maybe you could introduce me to a really good pub there."

This was a factor which would be a reoccurring element of my 10 year friendship with Cobb – good pubs and decent ales, both things I was very much drawn to myself. Indeed that first letter went on to recommend that I take my girlfriend to a number of bars in Tunbridge Wells when we were next there, including the 'Sussex Shades', behind the Pantiles where he knew the landlord - "an enormous bearded character who looked like a sea captain."

As you can tell from the fact that I am quoting verbatim from Cobb's letter it made a big impression on me and I have preserved it, and all the dozen or so letters and Christmas cards he sent me over the following decade.

I, of course, wrote back to him almost straight away after that first letter to set in motion a meeting down in Portsmouth. However, due to Richard's busy schedule this didn't actually happen until a Saturday in the middle of November 1986.

He again typed a letter to me, dated the 11th of November, letting me know he would be on the direct train from Oxford which arrived around 11.40am, although he wasn't sure which station he should get off at – Portsmouth or Southsea – though he choose Portsmouth as he imagined that's where the pubs would be rather than "genteel Southsea." In actual fact, the station in the centre of the city is Portsmouth & Southsea although the line carries on for Portsmouth Harbour to link up with the Isle of Wight ferries.

Luckily he did alight at the correct station and I was there, as promised, at the platform barrier to meet him. He was recognisable of course from the photo on the back of his books – although as he said in his letter: "I don't think you can mistake me for anyone else. I am pretty amazingly thin."

And he certainly was thin, especially compared to my corpulent self. Lindsey, when assessing photographs of him, referred to Cobb as 'The Tortoise', and indeed he did have the look of those wonderful creatures, without the shell of course. But despite being twig-like, he could certainly put away the beers, and I fairly had to pour him on to the train at the end of our first meeting after a pub crawl around the sites of Old Portsmouth.

Even though it was late in the year, the weather was very pleasant on that Saturday, and I remember sitting with Richard in the sunporch of the wonderful 'Still & West' pub, which jutted out into the channel of the harbour, supping Gales' HSB and talking about everything under the sun. He had very kindly bought me copies of two of his books, and wrote in one of them: "For Jon, a sunny day looking over the water".

Despite the near 50 year age gap, Cobb and I got on very well, helped, of course, by our twin love for decent beer. It was clear why his students had all loved him and how he had kept in close touch with so many of them. It was therefore inevitable that we would meet up again and he made plans for me to make a reciprocal visit up to Oxford one weekend the following year.

However, this would need to be in the summertime as Richard, with his wife, was off to teach at a university in South Carolina at the start of the new year for six months. Indeed, aside from a Christmas card, which told me he had got back OK from our first drinking session, the next letter I received from him was not until the start of June 1987 when he had returned from the US.

This time the letter was hand-written though, in his rather spidery way, because his typewriter had gone astray at

Gatwick airport on the trip out to America. He had turned 70 while away, a birthday which he said he enjoyed, saying "being 70 is so much more distinguished than being 69!"

He included a list of dates in June, July, or August for a potential meet-up, either in Portsmouth or Oxford, and said: "I'll have lots to tell you when next we meet (meet up in American, or meet with)."

I wrote back suggesting that I visit Oxford on August 8, and Richard replied – again in his spidery hand on the usual pale blue paper – that I should try and get there for 11am or midday so we could have a drink first in the 'King's Arms' before lunching in Merton College.

It was, of course, a very memorable visit, enlivened by copious pints of excellent ale and a pleasant lunch in the formal hall at Merton which was largely deserted given the absence of students, though I was introduced to a number of Dons, none of them as famous as my host.

A meeting that does stand out, however, was in the gardens of Balliol college as Richard took me on a tour of his Oxford. Strolling past us was the famous actor, Sir John Gielgud, and I could not stop myself from greeting him with a cheery, "Good day, Sir John", to which he kindly replied, "Good day, dear boy", smiling and quickly moving on.

Cobb was a little bemused, however: "Who was that old fruit?", he asked me, having caught the great actor's theatrical flare.

I looked at him rather strangely, naming the thespian and his achievements and mentioning that he had been in the TV adaptation of 'Brideshead Revisited', mostly set in Oxford, about five years previously. Richard, however, was not one for watching television, and had no real interest in the stage, so there was no real reference points to the theatrical knight.

Amusingly, as well, Cobb had himself just filmed a television appearance, having been invited to appear with Sir Harry Secombe on an episode of ITV's Sunday teatime show 'Highway' from Tunbridge Wells, being a famous citizen of the Kent spa town.

I had told him how great it would be meet the Goon Show veteran, but even that radio show meant nothing to Richard, for the understandable reason that throughout most of the 1950's when it was broadcast he had been immersed in his studies in France.

Cobb had written to me after the recording to say how much he enjoyed his trip to TW: "Harry Secombe is a SWEETIE, we stood outside Thackeray's house at the top end of the Common."

That programme was broadcast on 20th September 1987 and I wrote to Richard after telling him I had seen his brief appearance. He replied: "Yes, my appearance for the Secombe programme was both brief and unimpressive. Still, old ladies stop me in the street, on buses and in the post office, so I suppose I got some crumbs of reflected glory."

He added: "I quite liked Secombe as a person, but on the programme he did seem to sing rather much."

In this letter of October 1987 we were trying to organise another pub meet-up, this time in London as I was now living back – with Lindsey – at my parents house in the south-east suburb of Bromley. We had moved away from Portsmouth that summer as my now fiancee had got herself a job as a VAT Inspector with HM Customs & Excise in the neighbouring borough of Croydon.

I had given up the job I had eventually found down in Portsmouth – working for a small, and slightly dodgy mortgage brokerage in Cosham and then Southsea – and we had moved from the small basement flat we had been sharing for six months or so.

We had mainly got engaged because Lindsey's parents would not have tolerated us living together any other way – my own parents were pretty cool about it – and also because her younger sister had just got engaged, albeit to her childhood sweetheart with whom she had been going out for a long time. I'm afraid it wasn't a very romantic moment when I popped the question, over a can of tomato soup at lunch in our small flat in Allens Road. Lindsey had even had to pay for the engagement ring herself as I was borassic - she had seen a bargain she wanted and couldn't wait to wear it.

That flat was nearly as cold as Clarence Parade, even with the other two floors above still intact and occupied, with frost again appearing on the inside of the bedroom window during the winter. It was also memorable for the neighbour who occupied the flat above us and who would bang on his floor if our music was too loud. This culminated one Sunday evening with him stomping down to bang on our side-alley door and shouting at us to switch the noise off – to which Lindsey's response was to turn up the music, even though I told her not to do, although actually it was not that loud.

The neighbour continued to bang on the door, however, and managed to break the glass in it with his fist, cutting his hand. I then stupidly opened it to remonstrate with him, only to be grabbed by a powerful, muscular arm and dragged outside. Lindsey who was behind me screamed and said it was her radio and she would not turn it down.

The gorilla holding me, however, wasn't placated and said that as he would never hit a lady he would have to take it out on me as I cowered away from his looming fist. Eventually Lindsey saw sense and turned down the music and I was let go with a shove to the floor. The man stalked off and I crawled back inside and swiftly shut the door.

Luckily we had already given our notice at the flat and knew we would be moving a long away from this nasty neighbour, so we thought we could keep away from him until then. However, I wasn't to be so lucky. One evening later that week, having come home from work earlier than Lindsey I was greeted outside the flats by the gorilla who wanted to apologise for his behaviour, which he put down to a bad toothache. As a peace offering he invited me into his flat for a drink, which I was very loathe to accept but given the memory of the man's temper I decided I had better submit.

Inside his flat, this mountain of a man, poured out two large glasses of whiskey and told me to sit on a threadbare sofa as he went on to give me his life history. It turned out that although he was currently a bouncer at one of the Portsmouth nightclubs, he had previously lived in the east end of London and had alleged been an enforcer for the Kray twins. He had also spent some time in prison for Actual Bodily Harm – which didn't surprise me much – but was trying to go straight.

I managed to drop into the conversation that I didn't know much about the world of crime given that my father was a Police Officer, and made it out of the flat in one piece after about an hour and another large whiskey. Lindsey was waiting anxiously in the flat below having heard me talking to the main in the room above, but only asked if I had got him to pay for the new door glass! Luckily the landlady dealt with that herself and we managed not to have any further contact with the crazy neighbour, who perhaps was put off by the news that my father was in the police (I'd not said whether it was locally or somewhere else in the country). Interestingly, a few weeks later, when we had actually been away for the weekend, most of the other flats in the house were burgled aside from ours, which the landlady said was probably done by the gorilla to whom she had served notice to quit the building.

So by October 1987 we were living far from Portsmouth, but the connection with Cobb continued and we were to meet up twice more – in Beckenham in 1988, near my parents home, and then year later in Tunbridge Wells itself.

The meet-up in Beckenham took a while to organise, and was delayed from late 1987, because Richard had to have an operation on his right hand – luckily he was left-handed and still able to write, although by now he had got himself a new Olivetti typewriter.

Lindsey and I had moved out of my parents house by then and bought a little flat in South Norwood nearer our work in Croydon – for I had managed to get employment as a life inspector for the Scottish Provident Institution which was actually based in the same office building as Lindsey's VAT office.

The name of our block of flats was Ocean House, although as Cobb said in a letter "the Ocean does seem to be quite a long way from South Norwood (not that I am very sure where ANY Norwood is, is there a North Norwood?".

After another delay - "I am going to be a bit pressed with various bits of writing to finish while I still have two hands" – we eventually managed to meet up in March 1988, and I took the famous historian around to some of the haunts of my youth, visiting the more salubrious pubs in Beckenham high street.

That meeting was the last for quite a period of time as, aside from a Christmas card, there was no correspondence from Cobb for almost a year.

As he wrote in March 1989: "Sorry to have been such a rotten correspondent, but I have been overwhelmed with endless Bicentenaire stuff (it was approaching the 200th anniversary of the French revolution), conferences, lectures and so on, and last month I went back to South Carolina for a week."

However he was writing now to organise a meet-up for sometime the following month – typing that he was going to Caen for a week directly after Easter, and adding in pen 'via Portsmouth' – suggesting a "meeting place in an area where there are nice pubs".

He wrote again in April 1989 – "One day before Hitler's Hundredth Birthday" – to suggest Tunbridge Wells as a meeting spot sometime in early or late May. We agreed a date of May 27 and Cobb said he had "in mind a place on Mount Ephraim which is a pub-hotel and where I know we can get a good lunch".

Although, he added, "but we might have a pint at first in the 'Duke of York' in The Pantiles and we could even eat there."

I don't remember our Tunbridge Wells meeting as clearly as the other three, which is a pity as it was to be our last -

though I do know we did indeed stay in the 'Duke of York' for more than a few pints and lunch!

After that Richard and I corresponded fairly regularly but we never managed to arrange another meet-up, although in July 1989 he wrote that: "It might be an idea to have another session in TW (Tunbridge Wells)." But the pressure of getting a new book finished meant we never got anything organised, even though in a letter in late October he talked about dates early in December.

He explained: "I have been rather busy, with talks all over the place, but things seem to be easing off a bit now and this week I even hope to get back to a bit of writing for my new book. Now it is Winter Time, and I do like that."

I was at the time embarking on writing a part-time MPhil at the Polytechnic of Central London – soon to become the University of Westminster – having completed a two-year part-time MA there a few years earlier with my old mate 'Fascist' Mark from Portsmouth – who suggested it as a good excuse to meet up for a drink twice a week!

Richard was, of course, very generous with his help and advice, introducing me to 'Akenfield' author Ronald Blyth, who had written something on the topic I had covered in my MA dissertation, and to historian Ross McGibbon who he wrote was "a very nice Australian, and rare, for an Australian, rather shy."

That letter in October 1989 was actually the last I received from him, after that it was just a card at Christmas, usual with a short message scribbled in it.

In the card from December 1992 there was a longer note, however, enclosing his new address, for he and his family had moved from Oxford up to Whitby on the North Yorkshire coast.

"Alas!," he said, "Jonathon it will be some time before we can meet in The Wells. We've moved to NE8, are now installed mostly in the basement (which is <u>warm</u>) of this house (which isn't) in Whitby."

Cobb continued: "I feel quite a foreigner up here, the locals are friendly but I find it difficult to understand what they say. Mrs Gaskell was right in <u>North & South</u>, they are 2 different worlds."

He added: "I even looked into houses on sale in the Portsmouth-Southsea area, but they were all both pokey and expensive."

There was a final Christmas card the following year, in which Richard scribbled: "We hope to move back South away from awful Whitby in the course of 1994". But that was the last time I heard from him.

The next time I saw Cobb's name was when reading his obituaries in the middle of January 1996. There were many of them, of course, because he had a long life and many friends and former colleagues opined on it. I thought of writing with my condolences to his widow, Margaret, but I realised I no longer had an address for her, though I knew the family had moved back to Oxford where he died. I imagine as well she might not have looked too kindly on the young man who was leading her husband astray with pub crawls when he was in his seventies!

It was certainly true that we over-imbibed when together, but we did have some tremendous and memorable times, and I'm sure Richard was exactly the same with his other friends and family.

I was very blessed to have known him, even just for a short part of his later life, and I most certainly would have loved to have been one of his students either at the Universities of Aberystwyth, Leeds, or Oxford. He helped me to describe myself as a historian, encouraging me to continue studying and get my three degrees – one day, maybe, I will even attempt that PhD so I can be a Doctor too, like him.

And perhaps he even helped inspire me to write down these small memoirs of my life at Portsmouth Poly. In one of his letters, he lamented: "When are we going to get a novel about Pompey? Or even Southsea?"

These few words, I hope, provide some balm to that lament.

Afterwards – How I met the Belarussians

The railway station in Minsk, the capital of Belarus looked of little interest to tourists. Just another concrete scar on the face of a city remodelled in grey by Stalin in the 1950's, having been almost completely obliterated by the Nazis during the Second World War. Yet, underneath it, in the walkway to the other side of town, there was music emanating that drew me in to a growing crowd of people.

It issued from the smallest of battery-powered boom boxes, smuggled in from western Europe via the haven of West Berlin. The music was familiar - the husky voice of Nick Cave, the warble of the Cocteau Twins, the beat of something unidentifiable but far from unknown. The crowd also seemed familiar even though I'd never met any of them in my life. A mixture of twenty and thirty-somethings wearing jeans and t-shirts and all there for the same thing - to hear the latest sounds coming out from the West and hoping to get their hands on a tape or a CD that they could copy.

My friend Vladek, however, was far from unfamiliar to the crowd, and I was there because of him. He had on him a number of CD's that I had bought him from London. This was the currency that kept this illegal and chaotic music market going and as we walked through the underpass many people greeted him and questioned him about what he might have to offer. I couldn't understand them - the furthest my Russian, let alone my Belarussian could cope with was 'da', 'nyet' and 'spasibo!

We approached one of the boom-boxes set up on a upturned box and playing the Nick Cave album I had identified from the start. It was owned by one of Vladek's friends who was excited by the fact that I had bought over another of the great Australian's latest offerings -- 'Murder Ballads' I think - to add to this amazing barter system.

As he spoke to me in pretty good English - learnt like Vladek from late nights listening illegally to 'Voice of America' during the Soviet era - it was clear just how important the deliveries of these CDs from the West had been to him. Clear how I had made an important contribution to the musical life of these people just by having answered a personal ad in 'Q' magazine three years earlier. And clear how it had helped improve the cultural life of Minsk, and how it would change my life and perceptions forever.

Just to make it clear, I had never answered any other personal ad in my life. Not in 'Q' magazine, nor any other publication! What drew me to do so in the autumn of 1988 is still in mystery. I had been reading 'Q' from its launch two years earlier but would not have cited the personal ads as something I would even really have glanced at. Yet something had called out to me from one small-script advertisement.

Was it the address in a strange country I had hardly heard of; the plea for access to a world of rock'n'roll which I loved? Certainly the list of musical tastes mentioned coincided very closely to my own likes at the time - David Bowie, Brian Eno, David Bryne, Nick Cave, the Cocteau Twins. The mention of being able to receive in exchange some Soviet-era slabs of vinyl must also have excited my interest. I have always had an interest in Russian and Soviet history, nurtured by my mother's love of Russian literature, my own historical studies, and the romance of

David Lean's 'Dr Zhivago'. However none of that, of course, would prepare anyone for an insight in to life in 1980s Minsk.

The advert, I later learnt, had been placed in the magazine by David Ljunggren, a Reuters' journalist in Moscow who had met the man behind the Western CD/Soviet vinyl swap idea when he was studying the Russian language in Minsk around four years earlier. The mastermind of the scheme, Vladek Kasperchik had been DJ-ing in clubs that a number of the English exchange students had frequented in the early 1980s and struck up a number of friendships that helped keep his turntables spinning and expand his already encyclopaedic knowledge of the Glam Rock of the 1970s. Vladek was by day a chemist with two PhDs working at the Minsk Academy of Sciences - but his real love was, and still is, music.

David had been the first to introduce Vladek to 'Q' magazine, taking him an early copy when he went back to visit him in Minsk after his Reuters posting to Moscow, and it was exactly what he needed. Good reviews of everything that was being released in the UK, referencing it against similar sounds and influences. Vladek now could get a better idea of the modern Western music he might like; however he had no idea what it sounded like! Occasionally, some Polish radio station - only picked up if the atmospheric conditions were right - might play something he had read about, and David and other friends would bring him some CDs back from London, but they were sporadic. Then came the idea of the personal ad - a master stroke.

I wrote back directly to Vladek, as per the advert, detailing my tastes in music and asking what he would like me to send him first. This was going to be easy for me because I would get to buy CDs, tape them and send them on to him

- a great excuse to explain to my wife my increased record buying habit! I sent off my first batch of CDs in early 1989 and waited to see what would happen. Nothing it would seem for a while. This was not like a pen-pal arrangement. I didn't initially exchange details of my life in London in return for his in Minsk. It was solely about the music and I was intrigued by what Soviet vinyl I would receive in return.

I knew absolutely nothing about Soviet music. I did go out and find a very interesting book giving me some information on the rock'n'roll scene in the USSR in the 1970s and 1980s but of course my major problem was the fact that I did not speak the language. However, when the first batch of vinyl arrived in the post a few months after I had sent my CDs I was slightly disappointed. The main content was Soviet bootlegs of Western heavyweights, the Beatles and Deep Purple, and a classical album! This was what Vladek thought would be most accessible to me.

But it was the Soviet bands I wanted to listen to. There was one album of 70's Prog rock by a band called Alicia which, while being as dinosaur-like to me as Deep Purple, did excite some enthusiasm. I found out later that Vladek is around 8 years older than me and therefore his first influences were much more early 1970s, while mine were more punk and New Wave, things that had, not surprisingly, been passed by in the Soviet Union, being even more anti-social than rock'n'roll.

However a pattern was established. Every few months I would dispatch a batch of 3 or 4 CDs to Vladek, usually something off the initial list of around 100 albums he had sent me at the start, intermingled with something new I had recently enjoyed. Then a few months later a heavy parcel would arrive, tied up with string containing thick slabs of Soviet vinyl.

As time went by, Vladek tried out more modern sounding bands on me and although I still could not understand a word they were singing something in the music definitely grew on me. One of my favourites were a band from the far south of the Soviet Union called Kino. They had a sort of Joy Division feel to their music -- slightly grim but hypnotic. I later found out that the band's lead singer had been a depressive character who had been killed in the early 1980s in a seeming parallel to the life and death of the Manchester band's singer Ian Curtis.

Sometimes the parcels would go astray, with Soviet customs confiscating them more often than not. To combat this Vladek began building up a group of contacts who would take his parcels to London and take mine back to Minsk. Through groups like this I got to meet David Ljunggren for the first time and a number of other international students who had passed through the Belrussian capital and were co-opted into this postal service. More often than not I would receive a phone call from someone with a foreign accent asking me to meet them at Liverpool Street train station or Hampstead Heath after dark where we would swap parcels. I am pretty certain there must be an MI5 file on me somewhere as a result of this entirely innocent behaviour!

Then out of the blue, in September 1991, I received a phone call from Vladek. He and his wife, Irina were in London, staying with another of the Minsk student brigade who had also often brought over music for me, Neil Jenkins.

It was amazing they had arranged an exit visa. The Berlin Wall had come down late in 1989, and in August 1991 Belarus had declared its independence from the former Soviet Union, and was to become being one of the original signatories of the new Commonwealth of Independent States later that year. The early Perestroika in Belarus had allowed Vladek and Irina a travel window which they seized upon to make the journey to the UK to visit their many friends there for the first time.

Ironically, two days after they called, I was going to be paying a trip to one of the last remaining bastions of Communism in the world - China. So, at very short notice I only managed to meet up with Vladek and Irina for one evening in Neil Jenkin's flat in Swiss Cottage.

It was strange meeting up with two people I'd never met, in a person's flat that I had never visited, to have a meal cooked by someone who was completely over-awed by her first visit to a Western supermarket, especially as should could speak very little English. But with music as our guide we had an entertaining night and as a consequence of it I received an invitation for myself and Lindsey – who had stayed home packing - to make a visit to Minsk the following year. That was to be my first trip to the railway station music market.

Obtaining a visa to visit Belarus in June 1992 was fairly straight-forward, although as we were to be staying with Vladek and Irina we had to have an official letter inviting us to visit them. But it only took a brief trip to the Belarus embassy in London and a large-ish fee to get the permission. Our trip was to be a three centre affair, flying in to St Petersburg to stay with one of Vladek's friends, Nick for three days, then an overnight train trip to visit Minsk for three days; and another train journey to Moscow to visit Irina's brother, Sergei and see the sites of the Russian capital before finally flying home.

We had a magical time, seeing places I'd always wanted to visit, like the Winter Palace in St Petersburg and the

Kremlin in Moscow, and some I didn't know I wanted to visit, such as Minsk railway station. In St Petersburg we were driven around in a Lada by another of Vladek's friends, an ex-Afghan war veteran who kept a hand grenade in his car -- just in case! And it was only after we had been stopped by the police while driving back to Nick's apartment late one night that Vladek told us we were actually in Russia illegally, as we should have registered with the police and left them our passports overnight but our tight schedule meant that had been impossible.

After the first Minsk trip, I paid one more visit to Russia and Belarus a year later, on my own as Lindsey was then working in Paris for six months. This journey was even more hectic than the first, squeezing in trips to the same three cities and the train journeys in only one long weekend. But it was more fun as we had an amazing BBQ party in the woods outside Minsk and carried on to a party at the house of some other of Vladek's friends where I was drunk enough to try a 'Ukrainian Snickers'!

This is a Belarussian joke on their near neighbours consisting of a layer of raw pork fat -- stupidly I had mentioned that in the UK we eat pork crackling! - on a slab of chocolate. I can't say I liked the taste but the reaction on the faces of my hosts was priceless, and it is a story that is still mentioned whenever I meet any of Vladek's army of friends.

The most important part of my second visit to Minsk, however, was the fact that it would be my last, as Vladek and Irina had finally managed to obtain permission to emigrate to the USA. He had been to a scientific conference in Connecticut in the early 1990s and had been sponsored by a US businessman he met there.

The biggest wrench of emigration for Vladek, probably even more so than leaving his family, however, was what to do with his record and CD collection, the bulk of which he could not transport with him. The solution was to copy many of them on to tape and then persuade me to take these back to the UK with me in my luggage - around 6 boxes containing about 30 tapes each - which I could then take on to the US with me when (inevitably!) I went to visit him there.

The bulk of his CD collection was to be left in the couple's Minsk flat which his younger brother, Viktor took over. Viktor had good taste in Western music too, although his English was not very good, and I remember drunkenly walking back with him from the BBQ party in the woods singing Nick Cave's greatest hits.

At the end of my second visit, laden down with the cassette tapes there was a final memorable moment drinking Russian champagne from the bottle outside St Petersburg airport with Nick, before a bemused female customs guard questioned why I had bought all this music to the former Soviet Union in the first place!

I made it home with all of them, and a year later transported them again, this time across the Atlantic and to the other side of America, with Vladek and Irina having settled in a small town in Oregon. That trip was to be another life-changing experience for me - my first visit to the USA, a place before then I honestly had no real desire to visit (that would be my latent Communist past!) Of course Vladek had already started rebuilding his abandoned CD collection, by then and this time he had access to record stores!

Since my first trip to Oregon in 1994 I have visited Vladek and Irina a number of times and have fallen in love with the sights, sounds and comfort of holidays in the US of A. Vladek's CD collection has grown significantly, although now most of his music is stored on 3 hard drives in MP3 format - working for Hewlett Packard has broadened his technological knowledge – and now there is streaming!

I still get to meet many new 'Friends of Vladek' from around the world and knowing him has led me to make many other trips abroad myself, there was even a reunion trip back to Minsk 6 years ago.

Everytime I meet Vladek's friends they always ask me the same thing - how did we first meet? They realise that as I do not speak Russian I can not have been one of his student friends in Minsk. So, that's when I tell them the tale, about how an advert in a magazine changed my life.

Acknowledgements - A Sunny Day

I decided to scribble down these stories having been asked to relate one of them for the umpteenth time to the group of Polydrama friends I still meet up with every so often for drinks. So they are to blame – you know who you are: Adrian, Danny & Wendy, Russell and Susanne.

It was also an attempt to put my memories down before I start to forget them myself, and a way of actually finishing the writing of something. I have started so many novels, stories, and history pieces over the years but never complete anything. Maybe I have proved to myself that I can do it now.

Before completing these pages, I made my first trip back down to Portsmouth for probably twenty years. I had gone down many times before then, helped by the fact that my then in-laws had moved from Tunbridge Wells to the city where their daughter had studied to run a student guest house (of all things). However, post-divorce, there became no reason to relive those memories, and despite thoughts of celebrating big numbers like the thirtieth year of starting or finishing our courses at the Poly, nothing ever came of the plans.

But then I met up for a drink with Manf – sorry Chris – and he mentioned that he was still drumming in a band (having been the go to guy for all the student music outfits) and that they played a lot of gigs in and around Portsmouth, which was where their lead singer was from.

It turned out they were playing in a pub in Southsea just two weeks later and I resolved to go down and investigate my old haunts. I even invited all the Polydrama crew down as well, though given the short notice only one of them – Adrian – could make it.

He and I met in the 'Still & West' on a gorgeously sunny day in September, recreating my first Portsmouth pub experience almost thirty-four years on to the day, and my meeting with Richard Cobb at the end of it in 1986. After a pleasant lunch, we explored Old Portsmouth, bemoaning the loss of a number of pubs that we frequented, and then drove down to the pier – past the rebuilt flats on Clarence Parade – to lament the disappearance of even more of the bars and nightclubs we remembered.

It makes you wonder what students do for entertainment nowadays. But then given the debts they are racking up, and the course fees paid, they are probably all studying like fury rather than going down the pub every two minutes like we did – oh, I hope not!! My friends' children are just starting to go off to college themselves now, so I can only hope that they have as much fun as I did, as judged by these disreputable tales.

Anyway, Manf's band were excellent – check them out at lastecho.net – and they even played in a friendly pub I had never visited in Southsea: 'The Golden Eagle'. I walked the streets all round and found what I think were my other old flats – Shaftesbury Road, Western Parade, Albany Road, and Allens Road – but, of course, like Clarence Parade they have nearly all been done up now, and I didn't keep all the addresses.

I will hopefully go back to Portsmouth more frequently in future - maybe to see Last Echo again – and my memories will remain clearer now that I have committed them to paper.

I should also acknowledge those 'without whom' these memories would not have have been possible, of course, mostly especially my late parents, Kay and Dennis, my sister, Sian, and my niece, Bethany – who proudly continued my lead and did a nursing degree at the University of Bournemouth.

I will also mention Tricia, who one day will get working herself on scribbling something down on that expensive Apple Macbook!

JH 07/10/2017

Printed in Great Britain
by Amazon